30-DAY MARRIAGE MAKEOVER

DOUGLAS WEISS, PhD

SILOAM

Most CHARISMA HOUSE BOOK GROUP products are available at special quantity discounts for bulk purchase for sales promotions, premiums, fundraising, and educational needs. For details, write Charisma House Book Group, 600 Rinehart Road, Lake Mary, Florida 32746, or telephone (407) 333-0600.

30-DAY MARRIAGE MAKEOVER by Douglas Weiss
Published by Siloam
Charisma Media/Charisma House Book Group
600 Rinehart Road
Lake Mary, Florida 32746
www.charismahouse.com

Unless otherwise noted, all Scripture quotations are from the Holy Bible, New International Version. Copyright © 1973, 1978, 1984, International Bible Society. Used by permission.

Scripture quotations marked NKJV are from the New King James Version of the Bible. Copyright © 1979, 1980, 1982 by Thomas Nelson, Inc., publishers. Used by permission.

The testimonies of individuals in this book are fictitious and created from composites of clients who share similar issues. Names and identifying information have been changed to protect confidentiality. Any similarity between the names and the stories of individuals described in this book and individuals known to readers is coincidental and not intentioned.

Cover design by Gearbox Studio

Visit the author's website at www.drdougweiss.com.

Library of Congress Cataloging-in-Publication Data

Weiss, Douglas.
  30-day marriage makeover / Douglas Weiss.
      p. cm.
  Includes bibliographical references.
  ISBN 978-1-61638-140-0
  1. Marriage--Religious aspects--Christianity. 2. Spouses--Religious
life. I. Title.
  BV4596.M3W453 2011
  248.8'44--dc22

                                              2010041848

E-book ISBN: 978-1-61638-413-5

Portions of this book were previously published in *Intimacy*, ISBN
978-0-88419-767-6, copyright © 2001, and *The 7 Love Agreements*, ISBN
978-1-59185-724-2, copyright © 2005, both published by Siloam.

19 20 21 22 23 — 7 6 5 4 3
Printed in the United States of America

CONTENTS

Week 4: Making the Marriage Makeover Last

Introduction

GENUINE INTIMACY

GENUINE INTIMACY IS the cry of our nation. Many individuals search through multiple marriages trying to find the vital connection their souls long for. Still louder shouts the silence of the man or woman who has been married for decades and feels alone in that partnership. Many feel they have done everything right at home and with their spouses, yet there is little or no intimacy.

Far too many partners feel like roommates—as if they are just getting by emotionally. If fulfillment is promised, then why is it that few couples enjoy that impassioned connection? I don't think this is God's plan for your marriage. He wants you to live the abundant life and to have a marriage full of joy and love—and this is what we're going to accomplish these next thirty days. We are going to make your marriage over into what God has designed for you and your spouse.

I have lived in the laboratory of other people's marriages for many years. In addition, I myself have journeyed from the inability to be intimate to a place of deep intimacy and great fulfillment with my wife, Lisa.

Early in my married life I had the feeling that I was surrounded by walls. I desperately wanted to step out from behind those walls but could not find a way to connect to my wife. God in His graciousness drew me into the field of marriage and family counseling, where I gained much understanding. Still, no one explained, "These are the steps to intimacy:

1, 2, 3." The mystery of intimacy and the skills required to build and maintain it continued to elude me—as it does for so many others in my field.

It is in the laboratory of real marriage, real crisis, real love, and genuine desire for intimacy that we will solve the mystery. Part of the solution can be discovered in a series of principles that can be applied daily. I've counseled couples whose relationships were so distant that they had not enjoyed sex for more than a decade. When these same couples applied the principles in this book, within six weeks not only had they rekindled their sexual relationship, but also they actually started to like one other again for the first time in years.

Intimacy is really not a mystery at all—it is a process. Intimacy is the fruit of being in this process. Allow me to explain it another way: Wealth is a process. You work. You save. Maybe you invest. But to those who follow the basic principles of wealth and apply them, regardless of how they feel about them, wealth happens to them. The same applies to your health. Under normal circumstances, the process of eating right and exercising keeps you healthy. Those who do what they want, eat what they want, or spend what they want often do not achieve optimal health or wealth.

The same is true with intimacy. Those who do what they want emotionally with their spouse do not achieve optimal intimacy. The following pages will guide you into the process and the practical application of intimacy. Since intimacy is a process, I strongly believe that after thirty days of applying these skills, your marriage will be made over into a dynamic and satisfying relationship with so many benefits that you will never want to abandon these principles of living and the deeply satisfying intimacy with your spouse that they can bring—ever!

I have practiced these exercises in my relationship with my wife. Lisa and I have been married for many years, and as we have applied these principles to our marriage, we have continued to grow closer and stronger together. I believe the greatest gift to our children is a strong, vibrant, and lovingly intimate marriage. I wouldn't ask you to do something that I don't practice myself. Throughout the years, these principles have given life to my wife, to many of my clients, and to me. As you practice the power of intimacy, I pray that you and your partner will experience the abundant life that Jesus has promised each of you in your most intimate relationship—your marriage.

BEGINNING YOUR THIRTY DAYS

The next thirty days can breathe life back into your marriage, but you must work at it. Determine to spend this time mastering the basic skills necessary to enjoy satisfying and enduring intimacy with your spouse.

With Christian growth, those who pray, soak themselves in Scripture, have regular fellowship, and obey the Holy Spirit of God will enjoy intimacy with the Father. Disciplines are the structures of life breathed into us. This truth applies to intimacy in marriage too.

As you and your spouse take the next thirty days to commit to behaviors that support intimacy, your marriage can be completely transformed and made new—no matter what state it is in right now.

These thirty days are designed for the long haul. Remember, you are developing a marathon runner's mentality, not a sprinter's. So please take this next month seriously and discipline yourselves for the long haul. Happy training as you begin the happiest journey of your life—intimacy with your spouse.

During these thirty days you will begin to make over four key parts of a healthy marriage—spiritual, emotional, sexual, and making it all last for a lifetime. At the end of each day a place is provided for you to record your daily progress and make notes along the way. At the end of each week there will be a place to assess your progress for the week.

In the weekly section, space is provided for notes on three evaluation areas. You may write about your progress, such as whose date it was and the progress you are making on your financial structure. As you keep track of your progress, change will take place.

When your thirty days are completed, this book will be an enduring tool for developing and maintaining intimacy for a lifetime.

WEEK 1

THE SPIRITUAL MAKEOVER

THE THREE DAILIES— PART 1: PRAYER

I tell you that if two of you on earth agree about anything you ask for, it will be done for you by my Father in heaven. For where two or three come together in my name, there am I with them.
—MATTHEW 18:19–20

THROUGHOUT MY YEARS of counseling, I have discovered that many marriages lack structures to encourage intimacy. We grow up believing that one day we will get married and live happily ever after. We enter marriage ill equipped for intimacy and are disappointed when our husband or wife doesn't possess the secret code to intimacy either.

At first marriage is fun as you begin to learn about your spouse, go to work or school, get your first apartment, pick out furniture, go to church, and are physically intimate together without guilt. The sheer complexities of your new life together, along with the many new decisions you must make, can keep you talking and sharing regularly.

Slowly and subtly it happens. No one really knows when or where it happens, but something changes within the relationship. You don't seem to talk as much.

Decisions are not met with the same excitement as when you were first married; instead, they are delegated, then discussed. Purchases become fewer, and sex and life take on a routine. You don't feel as close but seem just to be living together. What happened? Where did the passion for one another go?

Americans believe that people are either passionate or they are not. But this kind of thinking is incorrect. Passion is a dividend of consistent investments made into a relationship.

Let's reflect back a minute to when you were dating. You were selling your spouse on the idea that being married to you was a great idea. Remember the passion you had for your future spouse? Of course you remember the passion, but what you may have forgotten is the foundation of that passion, the priority of the relationship.

Do you remember how you "made" time to be together? You planned your days and weeks around each other's work schedule, including your days off. Those of you who were attending school in another city away from your future spouse, as I was, had the phone bills to prove your passion and priority. In my case, those phone bills took a giant bite out of the little income I made just so I could tell her about my day.

If you were a Christian at the time, do you remember how spiritual you were? You prayed together as often as you could and perhaps even read the Bible together. You desired to know God's will, and you wanted God to help you stay pure and still express your love to one another.

Do you remember the gratitude you had for the smallest things your spouse did for you? This was especially true for me when Lisa cooked for me. I was so grateful! I filled her life with a constant stream of praise. Do you remember when you thought she was so smart and attractive and had so much potential? You believed in her and regularly encouraged her.

Understand that passion is a result of setting priorities. Too many people attempt to get back the *passion* instead of getting back their *priorities*. Once you get the priorities back, the passion follows and grows naturally.

What priorities? I will discuss priorities shortly, but before I do, I want to share an analogy I often use in counseling sessions. Many couples come in for help with sprains or fractures in their relationships. I liken the repair of a marital relationship to fixing a broken bone. When your bone is broken, you can continue to function in a limited way, but you look and act unusual. Then you go to the doctor or emergency room.

The first thing the doctor does is order an X-ray of the bone. Sure enough, he looks at the structure. Regardless of how it happened, the X-ray shows a damaged structure (your bone is broken). The doctor and nurse apply a structural treatment to your structural problem in the form of a cast.

The cast is a structural treatment that allows the bone to heal. The cast itself is just plastic or plaster, and it has no healing properties. But when it is applied to a broken bone to hold the bone in place, surprise! Healing can and does happen.

The same thing happens when you place the priorities back into your marriage. No matter how sprained or broken a marriage is, healing can and does take place. I have seen genuine miracles of restoration in marriages when priorities were put back into the relationship. One of the structures I apply is what I call "the three dailies."

I want to add a personal note of testimony. As I have stated before, I would never ask you to do something that Lisa and I have not done or are not doing presently in our relationship. Lisa and I have done two of the three dailies every day for years, with only a few exceptions. When I developed the third exercise, we actively applied it to our marriage routine also.

These three exercises help Lisa and I maintain our relationship priorities. They are part of our bedtime routine. Neither of us expects to go to sleep without our relational ritual of the three dailies.

They are a major highlight of my day. I get to hear about my wife's day, hear her heart, and she gets to hear about my day and heart as well. This relational structure has richly developed our skill for intimacy to such a level that it can weather the day-to-day challenges of children, writing, and media demands, together with all of our other commitments.

When your marriage priorities are restored, your passion will be restored. Everyone who knows me is well aware of my passion for Lisa.

I love her and really like her as well. This passion is the fruit of discipline that is born out of a heart of love.

THE THREE DAILIES

1. Prayer

Prayer is an absolute necessity in your marriage. I am constantly amazed when couples tell me that the last time they really prayed together, not including praying over food or a good night prayer with children, was years ago. Sometimes they say, "We both pray, just not together."

Psalm 127:1 says, "Unless the LORD builds the house, its builders labor in vain." The Lord must be part of building your house. Prayer is an active way to include the Lord as part of the building plan of your marriage.

Matthew 18:19 says, "Again, I tell you that if two of you on earth agree about anything you ask for, it will be done for you by my Father in heaven." As we've previously noted, this verse discusses the importance of two or more agreeing in God's name. It doesn't say when *one* agrees—it says when *two* agree.

Since Christ's resurrection, He intercedes with and for His bride, which is the church. The Lord sees prayer as being extremely important. God's pleasure is for us to commune with Him not just as individuals, but as a couple as well.

Prayer is one of the priorities that must be set in place by a couple desiring more intimacy. Remember, intimacy is three dimensional, involving spirit, soul, and body. As we grow together spiritually, our intimacy in the other two areas will grow as well.

Prayer is just talking aloud to God with your spouse, similar to talking with a friend. Prayer doesn't have to take long hours in any particular position. It is the principle of connecting with God that is essential.

As a couple, within your governing style in your marriage, process the decision of daily prayer. As a result of your decision as a couple, place a check by which of the following statements you agree with.

☐ We have agreed to pray daily together to improve and
maintain our intimacy for the next thirty days.

☐ We have agreed not to pray together daily for the next
thirty days, knowing that it will negatively affect our
intimacy.

The structure of prayer taking place within your marriage is one essential part of the three daily exercises. This structure will also be a part of your thirty-day log at the end of each day.

Hopefully you have agreed to daily prayer. I know better than most that each couple has many variables. Some of these differences include sleep preferences, work schedules, children's school and extracurricular activities, church, and fellowshiping with family and friends.

Look at your schedules. When can you pray together? In the morning? At lunch? In the evening? Take the time to discuss this with your spouse, and see if you can agree on a time to pray together. In the space below, write your first and second options to pray together.

Option one is _____ a.m./p.m.

Option two is _____ a.m./p.m.

In your thirty-day log, it's important to track your progress regarding this exercise to maintain the consistency that ignites the passion and intimacy you both desire.

Those who travel often ask how to maintain the thirty-day program while out of town. In this day of modern technology, it is a nonissue for the creative person. You can use your calling card or mobile phone to pray with your spouse over the phone. This really demonstrates a commitment to maintaining your spiritual intimacy. Even if you're in Hong Kong, you can e-mail a prayer to your wife and chat with her. Remember that the *structure* first brings healing, then passion. As you walk together spiritually, your intimacy over the next thirty days can flourish.

I love walking in the garden of my life with Lisa and coming with her into the presence of our loving Father. I really believe this has been instrumental in developing the strength and intimacy of our marriage.

Day 1

THREE DAILY EXERCISES

Pray together? _____ Yes _____ No

What did you pray?

_____

_____

Day 2

THE THREE DAILIES— PART 2: FEELINGS

A fool gives full vent to his anger, but a wise man keeps himself under control.
—Proverbs 29:11

EMOTIONAL INTIMACY IS the second very important aspect that couples need to develop and maintain throughout their relationship. Early in their dating relationship and then in marriage, they readily share with one another their feelings about life situations, people, God, and their dreams. Often they can't remember exactly what happened to their feelings a little later on, but many couples appear to go into hiding. Life gets more complicated, and their conversations get more managerial. Discussions become limited to, "Who does this? How will that get done?" or "That needs to get paid." There will be hundreds of details involving the children.

Your marriage can be managed and can function well and still not have the sense of connectedness that you once enjoyed. Eventually you can begin to feel alone, unsupported, and misunderstood, and you can end up wondering why you are even going through the motions. These feelings are common for couples who lack a system that supports each other's emotions.

14

When I talk with couples about expressing feelings, I find that many have limited communication skills. I can totally empathize. Even though I had hundreds of feelings, I only had three major doors of communication. This can get really fun if you marry someone with the same three doors.

I'm sure you have been in a conversation in which the feelings being expressed didn't line up with the real feelings the other individual was experiencing. We come equipped with many feelings, all of which are standard operating equipment placed in us by our Maker. The problem isn't that we don't have feelings. The problem lies in the limitations we have in the skills to express them.

When I was first married, I was emotionally illiterate. I had many feelings, but I lacked the skills to identify or communicate them to my beautiful bride, Lisa.

That's what identifying and communicating feelings is—a *skill*. Skills can be learned by anyone. Learning to do this is critical for intimacy. If you can't share the feelings in your heart because you lack training and practice, how can you expect heart-to-heart intimacy to occur? If you have been able to skillfully tell your spouse what you feel and what is in your heart, then your spouse must also be able to clearly communicate his or her heart back to you.

PUTTING IT INTO PRACTICE

Be warned that this communication exercise requires some effort to master. Over time the learning curve speeds up a little. Before you know it, you have it figured out, and you begin to feel a little more confident. In the end you will wonder how you ever got along before you learned it.

Consider what a wonderful day it could be when you truly know that you are completely heard and accepted by your spouse. This truly gratifying experience can be yours after time and practice.

The following exercise is designed to increase your ability to share your feelings with others.

THE FEELINGS EXERCISE

The feelings exercise is relatively simple. Pick a feeling from the list of feelings at the end of this day's reading. Place the feeling word within the following two sentences.

I feel _____ (feeling word) when _____.

I remember first feeling _____ (same feeling word) when _____.

Example 1:

I feel *adventurous* when I take my wife and two children hiking up the mountains in Colorado Springs.

I remember first feeling *adventurous* when I was about thirteen years old and my mom bought me a ten-speed bike, which I rode all over town.

Example 2:

I feel *calm* when I can get alone in nature and sit really still for a short while.

I remember first feeling *calm* when I was first taken out of foster homes and my mom gave me a stuffed animal that I could sleep with.

I think you get the idea. In the first sentence you pick whatever feeling you want and give a present-tense example of the feeling. In the second sentence you use the same feeling word but choose an early childhood or adolescent experience.

It is the earlier feeling that can be difficult. Do not cop out and try to give an example from a year or so ago. Think hard, and do the exercise correctly.

I want to warn you about two things. The first thing you don't want to do with this exercise is use the same feeling word over and over again. This really serves no purpose and will not create the desired effect for developing intimacy over the next thirty days.

The second thing you don't want to do in this feeling exercise is use one childhood example for twenty different feeling words. For instance, don't use the example of the child being left at the school every day with different feeling words such as *abandoned, helpless,* and *confused.* Although these feelings may be legitimate for one example, you must not keep pumping one experience over and over again when your life is full of experiences from which to identify your feelings. It may be slow going at first, but even childhood experiences become easier to remember when you practice the feeling exercise.

I have developed some guidelines to be used while completing this exercise. The following guidelines will limit or remove some obstacles that you might otherwise experience within this exercise. Please follow these guidelines to make your experience much more positive.

1. Don't use examples about each other.

You can talk about your feelings that include one another at any other time of day—but *not during the feelings exercise.* It is very important not to violate this guideline!

The feelings exercise is designed to be a safe place for both the husband and the wife to open their hearts to one another. If you start using the exercise to say, "I feel *frustrated* when *you* don't pick up your socks," the exercise will become unsafe and will dissolve. You can feel frustrated about traffic, your children, the dog, or anyone other than your spouse during this exercise.

This guideline applies to positive feelings about your spouse and not only negative ones. Suppose you use the word *cuddly*. Again, you can feel cuddly with the children or the dog, but don't use your spouse in the example during the feelings exercise.

This guideline is very important in order to keep the exercise alive and provide you both with a way to learn and maintain emotional intimacy.

You may choose two feelings from the list at the end of today's reading. Only do two feelings per day. Therefore, the wife does a feeling, and then the husband does his. Then the wife does her second feeling, and the husband does his second feeling as well. Then you're finished with the feelings exercise.

2. Maintain eye contact.

Look each other in the eyes while sharing your feelings. Looking into each other's eyes is important for intimacy to take place. There is much truth in the old saying, "Eyes are the window of the soul." When we look into another person's eyes, we see them.

As you and your spouse practice this exercise, eye contact will become increasingly natural. Many couples have experienced a significant breakthrough in their overall communication patterns simply by doing the exercise.

As you practice this guideline to the feelings exercises, I pray that you experience this kind of intimacy—one that transcends words.

3. Do not give feedback to your spouse.

As your partner shares his or her feelings, do not comment about the feelings he or she shares. This is critical to keeping the exercise safe for each spouse. When your spouse shares a feeling, pumping him or her for more information will not feel safe, and your spouse will be less likely to want to continue.

Another violation of the "no feedback" guideline would be suggesting that he or she "should not feel that way." Just accept what your spouse is saying. Don't interpret or comment verbally on what he or she has shared. Say thank you, and go ahead and share *your* feeling word next.

Follow the "seventy-two hour" rule. Whatever is shared during the exercise *cannot* be discussed for seventy-two hours. The reason for this rule is to give time for both of you to establish an emotional safety zone during this time. Intimacy, especially emotional intimacy, requires safety. You see, the feelings exercise isn't just about identifying and communicating feelings. It's thirty days of experiencing each other as emotionally safe people.

In a marriage in which a spouse feels emotionally unsafe, over time the partner will choose to stop being emotionally intimate. The need for emotional intimacy doesn't just go away for the spouse who doesn't share. He or she will seek out another emotional outlet. It may be golf with the guys, lunch with the girls, or a Bible study, but it won't be with the spouse. Over the long run, the emotionally vulnerable spouse can become receptive to emotional and sexual affairs.

After thirty days you can adjust the feeling structure. But stick to this structure for thirty days to gain the skills you need, and you will begin to enjoy what I call the *abundant marriage,* where you can be intimate spirit, soul, and body for a lifetime.

FEELINGS WORDS

Abandoned	Comforted	Fake	Irresponsible	Relaxed	Tense
Abused	Competent	Fascinated	Irritated	Relieved	Terrified
Accepted	Competitive	Feisty	Isolated	Remembered	Thrilled
Accused	Complacent	Foolish	Jealous	Repressed	Timid
Admired	Complete	Forced	Joyous	Repulsed	Tired
Adored	Confident	Forceful	Lively	Resentful	Tolerant
Adventurous	Confused	Forgiven	Lonely	Resistant	Tortured
Affectionate	Considerate	Forgotten	Lost	Respected	Touched
Aggravated	Consumed	Free	Loving	Responsible	Trapped
Aggressive	Content	Friendly	Lucky	Restless	Tricked
Agreeable	Cool	Frightened	Lustful	Rotten	Trusted
Alienated	Courageous	Frustrated	Mad	Ruined	Trusting
Amused	Cranky	Generous	Malicious	Sad	Ugly
Angry	Crazy	Genuine	Mean	Safe	Unacceptable
Annoyed	Creative	Giddy	Miserable	Satisfied	Unapproachable
Anxious	Critical	Goofy	Misunderstood	Scared	Uncertain
Apathetic	Criticized	Grateful	Moody	Scolded	Uncomfortable
Apologetic	Crushed	Greedy	Motivated	Scrutinized	Under control
Appreciated	Curious	Grim	Mournful	Secure	Understood
Appreciative	Dangerous	Grouchy	Nervous	Seduced	Undesirable
Approved	Daring	Grumpy	Nice	Seductive	Ungrateful
Argumentative	Dead	Happy	Numb	Self-centered	Unhappy
Aroused	Deceived	Hard	Nurtured	Self-conscious	Unified
Attacked	Deceptive	Healthy	Obsessed	Selfish	Unsafe
Attractive	Defensive	Helpful	Offended	Sensuous	Unstable
Awestruck	Delighted	Helpless	Open	Sexy	Unworthy
Badgered	Demeaned	Hesitant	Out of control	Shocked	Upset
Baited	Demoralized	Honest	Overjoyed	Shot down	Uptight
Battered	Dependent	Hopeful	Overpowered	Shy	Used
Beautiful	Depressed	Hopeless	Overwhelmed	Silly	Useful
Belittled	Deprived	Horrified	Pampered	Sincere	Useless
Betrayed	Desirable	Hostile	Panicked	Smart	Validated
Bewildered	Destroyed	Humiliated	Paralyzed	Smothered	Valued
Blamed	Different	Hurried	Paranoid	Sneaky	Victorious
Bored	Dirty	Hurt	Patient	Soft	Violated
Bothered	Disgusted	Ignorant	Peaceful	Solid	Violent
Brave	Disinterested	Ignored	Pensive	Sorry	Vulnerable
Burdened	Distressed	Immature	Perceptive	Special	Warm
Callous	Distrusted	Impatient	Pleasant	Spiteful	Weak
Calm	Distrustful	Important	Pleased	Spontaneous	Whipped
Capable	Disturbed	Included	Positive	Starved	Whole
Captivated	Dominated	Incompetent	Powerless	Stiff	Willing
Carefree	Domineering	Incomplete	Pressured	Stifled	Wiped out
Careless	Doomed	Independent	Pretty	Stimulated	Withdrawn
Caring	Doubtful	Innocent	Proud	Strong	Wonderful
Cautious	Dreadful	Insecure	Pulled apart	Stubborn	Worried
Certain	Embarrassed	Insignificant	Put down	Stuck	Worthy
Chased	Empowered	Inspired	Quiet	Stupid	
Cheated	Encouraged	Insulted	Ravished	Subdued	
Cheerful	Enthusiastic	Interested	Ravishing	Successful	
Choked up	Esteemed	Intimate	Real	Suffocated	
Close	Excited	Intolerant	Regretful	Sure	
Cold	Exhilarated	Involved	Rejected	Tainted	
Comfortable	Exposed	Irrational	Rejuvenated	Tender	

Day 2

THREE DAILY EXERCISES

Pray together? _____ Yes _____ No

What did you pray?

_____

_____

_____

Feelings exercise? _____ Yes _____ No

He shared _____

        (feeling #1)

   and _____

        (feeling #2)

She shared _____

        (feeling #1)

   and _____

        (feeling #2)

Day 3

THE THREE DAILIES—
PART 3: PRAISE AND
NURTURING

And he said: "I tell you the truth, unless you change and become like little children, you will never enter the kingdom of heaven. Therefore, whoever humbles himself like this child is the greatest in the kingdom of heaven."
—MATTHEW 18:3–4

THIS IS THE last of the three daily exercises you must practice with your husband or wife over the next thirty days. This exercise addresses the God-given need for nurturing and praise that each one of us has.

As parents, we intuitively know our children need to hear, "I love you," "I'm proud of you," "You're smart," "Great choice," and so on. I don't know where we get the notion that as we become adults we no longer need nurturing. We need to be mature, but we never are without a need for nurturing.

You are the primary voice in your spouse's life. A silent voice is cruel. The spouse who hears neither bad nor good from the husband or wife to whom they've committed their life feels hollow inside.

Both the giving and receiving of praise require skill. Again, a skill can be learned by anyone. Anyone can praise and nurture a soul. As you practice the praise exercise in this section daily, the oil of intimacy will drip into your soul and heal areas of dryness that you didn't even know existed.

When I counsel couples, I ask them, "When was the last time you received a real praise, eye to eye, heart to heart? Something more than just the obligatory, 'Thanks, honey'?" They look at each other and then shrug their shoulders. This is sad because this is the icing on the cake for me. Lisa tells me something positive about myself almost every day, and my soul leaps. I feel affirmed, and I can take on another day of life events. I know in the deepest regions of my heart that at the end of even the worst day of my life, those big green eyes of hers are going to look right into my heart, and she's going to say something nice.

Now I ask you, how hard do you think it is to be around someone who affirms you every day? Not difficult at all! We love to be around people who think we're special or praiseworthy. It feels even greater from your spouse.

Do you remember the biblical principle of sowing and reaping? If you sow praise, in time the harvest will come back to you.

The praise exercise is very similar to the feelings exercise. First, each of you individually must think of two things that you love, appreciate, or value about the other person.

The praises can relate to something your spouse did during the day or can simply be a general statement of appreciation for your spouse. When you both have two praises in mind, you are ready to begin this exercise.

Let's suppose the husband goes first. The guidelines for maintaining eye contact apply here as well. The husband must look into his wife's eyes and state his praise. For example: "I really appreciate that you are such a thrifty person, as in the way you saved us money by checking into mortgage insurance today."

The wife continues to look at her husband until she has accepted the statement or let it sink into her heart.

I said *heart* and not *head* on purpose. This is not a *cognitive* exercise but a *heart* exercise. After the wife has let the praise into her heart, she says, "Thank you."

Saying thank you is an important part of this exercise, for it indicates that the praise has been received. I used the word *received* because you may not agree with your spouse's praise at first due to the lack of skill in saying it well or your own feelings of inferiority. Nevertheless, you must still acknowledge that you let the praise into your heart.

At this time the wife would give her husband his praise. When he lets it into his heart, he then says, "Thank you." Then he gives his wife a second praise, and she gives him a second praise with the follow-up words, "Thank you."

For example: I will use the following praises and statements of appreciation that a couple named Trent and Natalie offered to each other. Trent will go first.

> Trent: I really appreciate the extra effort you made today in completing the decorating project.
>
> Natalie: Thank you.
>
> Natalie: What I really love about you is that you are sincere about working on our marriage.
>
> Trent: Thank you.
>
> Trent: I love the way you laugh. It brings me great happiness to hear your laughter.
>
> Natalie: Thank you.
>
> Natalie: I appreciate your making time for me at lunch today.
>
> Trent: Thank you.

This is how the nurturing or praise exercise sounds. It may seem simple, but for some it is difficult work. This exercise is sweet. When it is combined with the other two daily exercises, it can make a profound shift in your intimacy over the next thirty days. I am enjoying a lifestyle of both giving and receiving praise, and it has been great.

Take the time to process this exercise together. After discussing it as a couple, decide if this is something you would like to do daily over the next thirty days. Record your answers below.

☐ We are in agreement for thirty days to do two praises each daily.

☐ We are in agreement not to do praise on a daily basis.

These exercises will take time and work for each of you, but the work will get easier after ten days or so. Finding the time is going to be the most important part. As you both embark on the road to enhancing or maintaining your intimacy, you will need to set aside a time to practice these exercises.

In an earlier exercise you set a time aside to pray. Some couples do all three daily exercises at the same time to make it easier. When you become more skilled at them, all three exercises will take as little as ten to fifteen minutes each day. This is a very small amount of time to develop a vibrant, loving, and intimate marriage.

In the space below, record the time you both agree to make available to complete your three daily exercises.

We agree to pray, do two feeling exercises, and two praises each day at _____ a.m./p.m.

Our backup time is _____ a.m./p.m.

Wow! We've covered a great deal of ground on this day. I suggest that you become accountable over the next thirty days to a safe couple, a cell group leader, pastor, or counselor. Adding accountability increases your motivation to make it through the next thirty days successfully.

You can employ accountability by using something as simple as a telephone call to check in daily, or you can meet this person over lunch or at a check-in meeting every month. This person isn't supposed to give feedback or therapy. He or she is just there to hear about your daily progress on the three *pray, feelings,* and *praise* exercises. Decide together whom the accountability person will be.

Are you willing to do this for the next thirty days to intimacy? Record your findings below:

☐ We agree to meet with an outside accountability person for the three daily exercises over the next thirty days.

☐ We agree that if we miss more than three days of the three daily exercises, then we will implement an outside source of accountability.

☐ We agree not to have an outside accountability person for the daily exercises regardless of our progress over the next thirty days.

If you agree to have accountability to maintain the three daily exercises over the next period of thirty days, write down whom you choose. Also list a backup person in case you need one.

Our person or persons for accountability on the three daily exercises is _____.

Our backup person or persons is _____.

And that's it—the three dailies! I pray that for the next thirty days you allow this structure to teach you many skills. And I pray that these skills will become a permanent, positive part of your marriage. May God truly bless all the sowing that you are investing into your marriage, and may your good harvest be a blessing in which all of your generations can share.

Day 3

THREE DAILY EXERCISES

Pray together? _____ Yes _____ No

What did you pray?

_____

_____

_____

Feelings exercise? _____ Yes _____ No

He shared   _____

           (feeling #1)

    and   _____

           (feeling #2)

She shared   _____

           (feeling #1)

    and   _____

           (feeling #2)

Praise/nurture together? _____ Yes _____ No

He shared   _____

        (praise #1)

She shared   _____

        (praise #1)

He shared   _____

        (praise #2)

She shared   _____

        (praise #2)

Day 4

SPIRITUAL INTIMACY

In the beginning was the Word, and the Word
was with God, and the Word was God.

—JOHN 1:1

THE MOST UNIQUELY powerful picture of spiritual intimacy on the earth is revealed in the oneness of the Godhead, glimpsed through Scripture. The Word (Jesus Christ) and God were one in complete harmony, unity, and accord from the very beginning of time. That same oneness and togetherness are a part of God's will for us in our marriages.

I love reading the Bible and feeling the very keen sense that the author, the Holy Spirit, has intimacy as a personal objective for its readers from beginning to end. God made man and woman in the garden not only to fellowship with each other but also to fellowship as a couple with Him.

In the beginning God walked with Adam and Eve daily—until sin severed the union. Imagine as a couple having God the Father teaching you to love, commit, and feel equally loved and understood. But the Holy Spirit does not leave us only with the picture of how God intended intimacy to be. He also pens a great word picture of Christ and the church.

The picture is of the hero and Savior, the Lord Jesus Christ, who lived

29

and died for His bride so that she might be with Him forever. This word picture closes with Jesus coming back for His bride and hosting a great banquet to celebrate their eternal intimacy.

God is a romantic, and He is definitely interested in the issue of intimacy. That is why it is so important that we begin this study about intimacy by reflecting on the scripture "In the beginning was the Word, and the Word was with God." Without God, intimacy is short-lived and incomplete. Even if it were possible for a husband and wife to achieve emotional and physical intimacy, their lives would feel incomplete without spiritual intimacy—living as individuals and as a couple in relationship with the all-loving God.

My personal spiritual journey started with the love of God being poured into me through the salvation of our Lord Jesus Christ. Without His consistent love and gentleness, I would know of nothing to write on these pages about intimacy. He is my greatest teacher on giving and receiving love and intimacy.

The scripture that declares this message loud and clear to me is Psalm 127:1: "Unless the LORD builds the house, its builders labor in vain." This can be no truer than for the couple who desires intimacy within their marriage without actively involving God in the process. As this scripture indicates, they would definitely be laboring in vain.

You may be a born-again Christian believer. But you may be someone who has never accepted the love of God into your life.

If you have never encountered God personally, I encourage you to take a moment and ask Jesus Christ to show you His love and His forgiveness for all the sins that have separated you from Him. Only then will you experience true intimacy from the master of intimacy Himself, Jesus Christ.

Nevertheless, spiritual intimacy is not an automatic attribute of all who believe. I have spent countless sessions with believers who don't understand even the basics of spiritual intimacy. Some individuals and couples struggle painfully with the concept of intimacy with the Father.

For this day, I will outline some of the basics of spiritual intimacy for individuals and couples.

HONESTY IS THE ONLY POLICY

Honesty is so basic to spiritual intimacy that I must address it as the first issue. Intimacy can never be increased where dishonesty and deception exist.

Many individuals have what I call an "image relationship" with themselves. They work at crafting their image so much that they themselves buy it hook, line, and sinker. Such image crafters usually focus on the wonderful parts of themselves, such as their gifts or shining qualities. Their self-styled image may be charismatic, outwardly displaying wonderful virtues such as caring, sincerity, spirituality, and intelligence. They often appear nearly perfect.

When I was a young Christian in Bible college, I couldn't even walk out of the dorm room unless everything matched. I was quite an image to behold—a young, clean-cut, well-dressed Bible school student and choir member. Nevertheless, I only had an image relationship with myself. I was completely unaware of my real heart condition or even how I truly felt. I appeared righteous and was always ready to convince anyone that I was OK. The only problem was that I wasn't real. I was well schooled in all the religious rhetoric; I could spout off dozens of memorized Bible verses to fit the moment, but I couldn't have a relationship to save my life.

What does this have to do with spiritual intimacy? Everything if you're a Christian desiring intimacy. In truth I was a hurting human being who used religion to protect my heart, and it took God years to tear down that self-image so that I could begin to experience genuine intimacy.

Self-honesty is very important. Not one of us human beings is perfect or even close to it. If you take any one of us away from the normal comforts of daily life and place us in an unusually stressful situation, such as an all-day layover in an airport or being stuck in bumper-to-bumper traffic, less than wonderful things will often come out of our hearts.

It's absolutely wonderful to be human, isn't it? We are imperfect by our very design. If we could be perfect, then we wouldn't need a Savior, would we? Growing beyond false religious images and discovering who you really are is just the beginning of spiritual intimacy.

Are you thinking that this really doesn't apply to you? Try this exercise to find out. Think of your three greatest flaws. Now take a minute and come up with seven more. I find that in doing this, many of us can come up with one or two—but ten? Who even imagines that he could have ten faults? Take a moment at this point and write down ten of your worst faults and see how long it takes.

The longer it takes for you to come up with ten faults, the more important self-honesty is going to be for you on your journey toward spiritual intimacy with your spouse. By the way, when you're writing down these faults, don't cheat and ask your spouse to help.

Honesty about how you feel, honesty about your perceptions, and honesty with who you are, are central to spiritual intimacy. As you go through the various exercises in this book and the three dailies, you will begin to discover more and more about the real you than you may have thought possible.

The great news is this: You won't be doing this alone. God will be with both you and your spouse, walking together with you throughout this journey.

Recently at a lunch meeting a woman asked me how a man could be taught to see the real beauty of a woman when he first meets her. I responded that it was not possible. How can you appreciate the complex caverns of a woman's soul at a moment's glance? It takes a journey of decades for a man to behold the beauty of a woman. The fragrance of a woman's many passions for life, love, and relationship; her waves of emotion; and her valleys of woundedness and fear could never be understood during a superficial encounter.

Intimacy is an exciting journey with a wonderful destination. The adventure of intimacy's discovery makes the traveling so much fun for you and your spouse. Honesty is one signpost on the way to spiritual intimacy. You must be honest with yourself, with God, and with your spouse.

IT TAKES WHOLEHEARTED COMMITMENT

Like honesty, intimacy also requires commitment to yourself, to God, and to your spouse. Intimacy rarely happens by accident, and it is even rarer that it can be sustained over a lifetime without genuine commitment.

I am personally very committed to intimacy. At times I think I wear my wife, Lisa, out about it. I want to know her thoughts, feelings, beliefs, and fears. I want to savor the scent of her personality, the moments of her fury, and the playfulness of her spirit. I am committed to intimacy with both my God and my wife—and this commitment is not half-hearted. You can look into my life to see that my behavior supports my commitment to spiritual intimacy.

Truth is always easily found in a person's behavior; that's where an individual's commitment will always show up. For me it's one of the things that makes working with people so much fun. A person who wants to lose weight designs a plan and then follows through. A person seeking wealth plans to earn, save, and invest to reach his or her goals and then works the plan. Spiritual intimacy is not any different. An individual who wants to experience spiritual intimacy with both God and a spouse can create a plan. As he or she follows through, the level of commitment will be revealed in the outcome.

Intimacy on all levels requires commitment, whether it be spiritual, physical, or emotional. No amount of reading about intimacy can give you genuine intimacy. You must make a commitment and then follow through with it.

As you walk through the various aspects of intimacy, your commitment will be challenged. Your determination to follow through will become an essential tool in obtaining the intimacy you seek. In the next thirty days, as you and your spouse complete the exercises offered in this book, your entire life can be dramatically changed.

It will take focus, commitment, and hard work, but in thirty days I believe you can experience intimacy on every level and maintain this intimacy for the rest of your life together.

Day 4

THREE DAILY EXERCISES

Pray together? _____ Yes _____ No

What did you pray?

_____

_____

_____

Feelings exercise? _____ Yes _____ No

He shared _____

       (feeling #1)

and _____

       (feeling #2)

She shared _____

       (feeling #1)

and _____

       (feeling #2)

Praise/nurture together? _____ Yes _____ No

He shared _____

(praise #1)

She shared _____

(praise #1)

He shared _____

(praise #2)

She shared _____

(praise #2)

Day 5

BUILDING YOUR HOUSE

Unless the LORD builds the house, its builders labor in vain.
—PSALM 127:1

S PIRITUAL INTIMACY IS the cornerstone upon which all genuine intimacy can be built. That's why it is the cornerstone of this thirty-day guide to a new marriage.

Spiritual intimacy can be broken down into two categories: personal intimacy with the Father and marital intimacy with the Father. Let's investigate.

THE FIRST STEP OF PERSONAL INTIMACY

Spiritual intimacy begins in an intimate relationship with Jesus Christ. The temptation to be religious, to practice religious forms and expressions devoid of genuine relationship, is ever present in all of us. Intimacy is never about religion—it is never a list of dos and don'ts. Intimacy only arises from a dynamic connection to the living person of God through Jesus Christ.

No one on this earth can tell you how much food makes you full. It doesn't even seem rational. Could you imagine going to a restaurant, and two-thirds of the way through your meal your waiter stops you and says, "Excuse me, but you're full, so stop eating now"? Is that not the most ridiculous thing you have ever heard? I certainly know when I am full, and I know when I am hungry. It's funny, but when I am hungry I can act a little differently.

Here's my point: no matter how sincere or knowledgeable a spouse, teacher, or Bible scholar may be, they can never tell you how much prayer, Scripture reading, or praise and worship of God you need on a daily basis to be full; they can only encourage you to eat enough.

Therefore you must ask yourself, "Is my spirit being fed enough through worship and praise, prayer, and God's Word to be filled?" I can't tell you how much is enough, but you do need to eat daily from God's banquet to maintain spiritual intimacy. So if you're spiritually full most days, great! But if you're spiritually hungry and acting selfish, rude, or impatient, then you may need to make some changes. Examine yourself. What is the fruit of your spiritual tree? Galatians 5:22–23 says, "But the fruit of the Spirit is love, joy, peace, patience, kindness, goodness, faithfulness, gentleness and self-control. Against such things there is no law."

From personal experience I can tell you that I need to have intimacy with God daily in my life to maintain intimacy with my wife. My flesh loves to be rude and selfish, so I need a certain balance of worship and praise toward God along with prayer and meditation on His love letter to me (the Scriptures).

Make a plan to feed yourself daily. Remember, it's not *religion*; it's *relationship*. No person needs to preach me into eating lunch! When I get hungry, I eat! So commit to behaviors that make you spiritually full. Don't be like the man in Proverbs 19:24: "The sluggard buries his hand in the dish; he will not even bring it back to his mouth!"

Imagine that you're dining in a fine restaurant. The gentleman at the next table has a wonderful meal laid out in front of him, but he is too lazy to put the food in his mouth. Wouldn't you wonder what in the world was wrong with him? To top it off, you learn that the fabulous meal was *free*! He didn't even have to pay for it to eat it. He simply had to eat.

I think you get the point. Jesus Christ paid the price of spiritual intimacy for us all. Every day He prepares a banquet of spiritual delights so that we can be filled. All we have to do is show up and eat. I encourage you to a make a plan for yourself so that every day you can be filled through the spiritual intimacy that was freely given. Eat up—it's free!

MARITAL INTIMACY

Much like personal spiritual intimacy, marital intimacy requires a commitment from each spouse to work together spiritually. God walked with Adam and Eve in the garden. He did not walk with just one of them but with both of them jointly. As we saw earlier, this is also true of the Godhead. John 1:1 says, "In the beginning was the Word, and the Word was with God, and the Word was God." Togetherness and spirituality are truly concepts that are linked in the Bible.

Do you want to take a spiritual journey with God the Father and with each other? As we've noted, the first step in this togetherness concept is commitment. But don't think ahead to the practicalities and methods of this commitment just yet. Doing so might only serve to stir up religious fears. Instead, just tell each other how committed you are to spiritual intimacy in your marriage.

At this point take a moment to close this book and talk to your spouse about spiritual intimacy. Don't merely address methods; instead, affirm your commitment to each other and to spiritual intimacy. Since spiritual intimacy is the cornerstone, don't proceed any further until you have both agreed to take this journey together. Use the chart below to record the results of your conversation.

MARITAL SPIRITUAL INTIMACY

Count me in on marital spiritual intimacy. I don't know what we will do yet, but I am committed.

He said: Yes   No   She said: Yes   No

Today's date: _____

It's important that both spouses agree to marital spiritual intimacy before a plan is designed to implement your goals. The Bible says, "Do two walk together unless they have agreed to do so?" (Amos 3:3).

Now that you both agree to be committed, you can work out the details together later on when we offer practical suggestions for you as you take this intimate journey with God and your spouse.

Perhaps you haven't prayed together in years or maybe decades. Maybe you have sat side by side at church together for years but have never opened a Bible together. No matter where you are in your relationship, with God all things are possible. Choose to be optimistic, to believe that God desires genuine, satisfying, and delightful intimacy for you and your spouse. Later on you will begin to learn how to walk out your commitment.

Intimacy has been an awesome discovery as I've experienced God and my wife, Lisa—who is God's precious daughter. I love growing together spiritually as a couple in the exciting adventure of intimacy.

Day 5

THREE DAILY EXERCISES

Pray together? _____ Yes _____ No

What did you pray?

_____

_____

_____

Feelings exercise? _____ Yes _____ No

He shared   _____

                  (feeling #1)

    and   _____

                  (feeling #2)

She shared   _____

                  (feeling #1)

    and   _____

                  (feeling #2)

Praise/nurture together? _____ Yes _____ No

He shared   _____
              (praise #1)

She shared   _____
              (praise #1)

He shared   _____
              (praise #2)

She shared   _____
              (praise #2)

Day 6

THE PRINCIPLE OF AGREEMENT

Do two walk together unless they have agreed to do so?
—AMOS 3:3

ANYTIME A HUSBAND and wife are making a decision on how the couple or family system is going to operate or on what foundation they will build their house, it is important to consider the principle of agreement.

Every couple develops a system of governing. Some couples choose a *theocracy*, in which God is the head of the family. Both spouses are subject to Him and seek Him for wisdom and guidance. Neither person holds all the truth or all the power. Instead they both respect Christ in each other and accept that as a team they hear and obey God.

Other couples knowingly or unknowingly choose a *monarchy*. This is a popular system in which one person (often the husband) has the ultimate deciding power. He is the king of the family. The king may be a benevolent king and one who humbly listens to the wisdom, perspective, and feelings of his spouse. He may truly seek God and base his decisions on the Word of God, prayer, and the guidance of peace through the Holy Spirit.

But on the other hand, the king may not be a humble king. He may be proud, selfish, or even addicted to something. His ability to glean insight from his spouse may be limited, or doing so may be irrelevant to him. His spiritual maturity may be limited or even nonexistent, although he may attend church.

Another system of government that a couple may choose to decide upon could be a *democratic* system. In this system, at least hypothetically, each partner has a 50 percent vote or ownership in the marital system. Each couple makes his or her positions, arguments, and feelings known. Each spouse feels he gets to express his positions on the matters at hand. If they disagree, they can stay in a gridlock of arguing and positioning until they agree or until the person with the most emotional energy around the issue succeeds.

Again, if both spouses include Christ in their decision-making process and seek God and His Word, this system can operate peacefully—some would say successfully. Both spouses have and give respect to each other. Both are listened to, and once a decision is agreed upon, both accept responsibility for the outcome.

However, if the spiritual maturity of one or both partners is limited or nonexistent, this system can become volatile. Continual manipulation, control, and personality- or emotion-based rationales and entitlements can disrupt this style of governing quite significantly.

A last system of government is a *corporate* governing style. This couple actively agrees upon areas of responsibility. They create two department heads or two vice presidents. In this system, one department may be fully responsible for outside of the house decisions such as the yard, lawn, or vacations. The other spouse may be responsible for all the decisions on the interior such as the utilities, decorating, and managing the shopping. They set up corporate policies on spending and have mandatory meetings when spending more than a certain amount of money.

The department head does have unilateral decision-making responsibility over his department. He or she does not need to consult the other spouse unless a particular expenditure demands a business meeting by both departments. The greatest difficulty with this system is deciding who is responsible for what, including child-care issues. Once the corporate structure is set up and agreed upon, the system can run smoothly.

Like the previous system of governing, the success of this system depends upon the level of spiritual maturity of each department. If both are reasonably mature, this system can make for peace or harmony inside a marriage. Some couples choose this system from the beginning of their marriage, and others evolve into this system as their lives become more difficult to manage.

It's important to examine major governing themes because in money issues (discussed more thoroughly in the last section of this book), the couple's true system of government will be exposed immediately. As a marriage therapist, anytime we move into the issue of finances, the couple's real beliefs and behaviors become obvious to all three of us in the room.

One of the best ways I know to illustrate this is with the example of a couple who is deciding to buy a new car. They may both weigh the issue of whether or not to buy a car now. If they decide to buy a car, whose car is it, and who decides what kind and color it should be? If one or both go to buy the car, then who handles the insurance issues, and who takes care of the ongoing maintenance of the vehicle?

In the theocratic system, both partners will sincerely pray individually and as a couple, and then go through the entire car-purchasing process seeking God's will first. In the monarchy system, the king will decide when and what to buy, perhaps choosing to delegate all the details. If he is a good king, he may seek God individually for His will on a vehicle purchase.

Within the democratic system the husband and wife may "discuss" this purchase in great detail, vote, and agree on each part of the process. If they are Christians, we would hope they would involve God, His Word, and prayer in the process.

In a corporate system of governing, it is the person who is in the department who makes the decision in the case. The couple agrees on whose department it falls under, and that person makes the decisions. If he or she is a loving department head, he consults the other department (his/her spouse) during the process. The department head can, however, by the power delegated to him by the corporate structure, make unilateral decisions for the company (marriage) and purchase a vehicle that seems appropriate to him.

The principle of agreement comes into play when the husband and wife actively decide their governing style. Agreement is often lacking in immature, youthful marriages, but marriages evolve into this process as a couple grows.

Now, as adults, it's time to really decide how to govern yourself. You will need to set aside some time for several discussions in order to work through this process. Both spouses must make decisions without manipulation in order for the agreement to be official.

If you neither decide on a system of governing nor participate in one, you may be setting up roadblocks to intimacy. We are seeking to remove obstacles that hinder the intimacy God desires for His children to have in a marriage. If you and your spouse fully agree on a governing system, peace can reign in a marriage regardless of the particular system you choose. As we say in America, "The people have spoken."

Smoother sailing can be ahead of you than the waters through which you have navigated in the past. If the organizational chart is clear, many decisions can be made without disrupting your marriage. The more peace there is in this area of your marriage, the greater the chance your marriage has at maintaining and growing in intimacy.

CAST YOUR BALLOT

After hours of consideration, the hour of reckoning is come. The clock is striking twelve, and the streets are clearing as both husband and wife place their votes as to how they will govern. This is a historic event. Please fill out your governing papers.

Pertaining to the marriage of Mr. _____ and Mrs. _____, we hereby certify and agree to govern ourselves primarily in a _____ form of government. Let it be hereby known by community, church, and our Lord Jesus Christ that on this date of _____, we both agree without duress to conduct our governing decision-making process accordingly until further decreed by the sovereignty of our marriage. We do so by the power invested in us both by our God and by the state of _____ in holy matrimony.

Wow! I feel better already. Once you as a couple agree on the governing style, so much stress can be relieved. There are so many decisions to be made over the decades of your marriage that it is of paramount importance that you agree on a process for these decisions.

Day 6

THREE DAILY EXERCISES

Pray together? _____ Yes _____ No

What did you pray?

_____

_____

_____

Feelings exercise? _____ Yes _____ No

He shared   _____
                 (feeling #1)

    and   _____
                 (feeling #2)

She shared   _____
                 (feeling #1)

    and   _____
                 (feeling #2)

Praise/nurture together? _____ Yes _____ No

He shared   _____

(praise #1)

She shared   _____

(praise #1)

He shared   _____

(praise #2)

She shared   _____

(praise #2)

Day 7

THE MARITAL HOLY OF HOLIES

I will praise You, for I am fearfully and wonderfully made;
marvelous are Your works, and that my soul knows very well.

—PSALM 139:14, NKJV

THE WORLD WE live in is definitely a physical one, and God certainly knew what He was doing when He created Adam and Eve. He made these crowning masterpieces of His work to be able to walk, talk, taste, smell, see, and hear the physical world He created for them.

The physical world is a great place. I love to climb the mountains, see the jagged rocks and icy brooks, and smell the pines in Colorado where I live. I love the fact that I can hug and play with my children.

I realize that the physical world has its limitations since sin entered the world through Adam. We have sickness, diseases, and just plain old bad days because of the bodies in which we live. Still, our bodies are a wonderful gift for experiencing intimacy with our spouses.

NONSEXUAL INTIMACY—THE POWER OF TOUCHING

We can experience incredible intimacy through the thousands of nerves placed in our physical bodies. Each of us needs to be hugged daily to

49

feel good about ourselves. Touch is so important that infants who lack physical affection do not thrive.

Psychologists generally agree that as humans we need—not just want—physical touch. Nonsexual touch is extremely important.

This is especially true in a marriage. A couple who regularly touches one another by holding hands, hugging, kissing, and giving an occasional pat on the back has mastered this much-needed nonsexual physical intimacy. Even men need to be hugged, kissed, and enjoyed physically by their wives.

Did you grow up without any of your physical intimacy needs being met? Many people do. If so, you may have a deficit in the area of physical touch, as well as a skewed perception of the value of physical touch. Fortunately, God often puts an individual who hasn't been touched together with a spouse who likes to be touched and likes to touch. This gift is not always received well and can even be a source of contention. This was exactly the case in the following story.

Mary Alice is a fifty-six-year-old secretary who has worked most of her life. She grew up in a Mennonite home in Pennsylvania where everyone did his chores, got good grades, walked the straight and narrow road, and, of course, went to church. She really couldn't remember hugs or kisses from her family as she grew up.

Mary Alice worked in a local office in town and met Daniel, a fine Christian man who sold insurance. Danny, as everyone called him, grew up quite differently. He was hugged, touched regularly, and kissed often, even throughout his teenage years. Hugging Mom, Dad, sister, or brother was normal for Danny.

Danny and Mary Alice fell in love and married after a couple years of dating. Soon into the marriage it became obvious that they thought very differently about physical intimacy. Sex was OK with Mary Alice because she believed that was her Christian duty toward her husband, but she wanted no part of Danny's desire to hug, kiss, and be playful.

If Danny hugged Mary Alice, she froze up. When he kissed her, not only would she not respond, but she would actually recoil also. She could not initiate a spontaneous touch, hug, or kiss toward Danny. He didn't understand his wife's coldness; however, he knew that she loved him.

Three years went by, and Mary Alice told him that she felt the only reason he hugged her and wanted her attention was for sex. Although he adamantly disagreed, she sincerely believed she knew "the real truth." After their second child came along, Danny gave up trying to be physically close with his wife. He stopped asking for hugs and kisses and was no longer physically playful. He was faithful to her, but deep down he began to get angry.

He told me, "I felt an ache I couldn't get to." He got massages occasionally at the health center, which seemed to scratch his itch to be touched for a while, but the anger didn't go away.

Danny stayed married, stayed faithful, and stayed mad. He had been experiencing touch deprivation for almost three decades and felt increasingly vulnerable to get into an affair in order to get his touching needs met.

His issue wasn't sex; it was touch. Through counseling, Mary Alice was convinced to try nonsexual touch. Under the guidelines that Danny could not use it to initiate sex, she felt safe to experiment physically. Eventually Mary Alice not only accepted Danny's need for legitimate nonsexual touching, but she also began to discover her own needs for touch as well.

Mary Alice made the turn when she realized, "Why should he get all the touching? What about me?" This couple was on their way to restoring physical nonsexual intimacy. Danny was genuinely grateful for the spontaneous kisses of his wife. Mary Alice repeated to me what he told her: "My husband wants to say thank you for giving him a new wife." We laughed and thanked God for the healing that took place in their lives.

Touch deprivation is painfully real today in marriages. Some couples touch only during sex. How sad when God has given us the wonderful gift of our physical bodies with which to enjoy each other. Touch is a great way to express intimacy. Fewer things are better than a time of cuddling or massaging or scratching your spouse's back.

Physical touch is important not only for your marriage but also for the quality of your children's marriages. Are you modeling the kind of affection to your spouse that you want your sons and daughters to give and receive in their marriages?

At this point, evaluate the place physical touch has in your relationship with your spouse. Spend some time together discussing your answers.

1. Is physical touch mostly associated with sexual advances?

2. Do you have consistent patterns of hugging, holding hands, and kissing?

3. Do you ever just hang out and touch each other?

4. Does one person give much more touch than the other?

5. Does one person do almost all the initiation of touch?

6. Have your children laughed lately because of a spontaneous show of your affection to your spouse?

7. Is touch a much-needed area for improvement in your marriage?

8. Are you committed to working on physical touch in your relationship for the next thirty days?

SEXUAL INTIMACY—THE MARITAL HOLY OF HOLIES

Sexual intimacy is the ability to engage your spouse spiritually, emotionally, and physically. It is the holy of holies of your relationship. Sexual intimacy allows us to know and be known in a way that no other person knows us.

Sexual intimacy can be the greatest connection that a man and woman can experience here on this earth. This pleasuring and exploring of each other is God's will and God's design.

Have you ever thought about the thousands of changes your body goes through during the sexual act? Your organs become enlarged, fluids exchange, nerves are excited, and pleasure is experienced at an almost traumatic rate. God designed this. He designed our bodies so that we could enjoy the ultimate pleasure within a marriage. This was His idea, and I personally think it was one of His better ones!

Sexuality is such an integral part of who you are. Sharing yourself physically, emotionally, and spiritually is the deepest level of intimacy that you can experience with your mate. Sexual intimacy is the ultimate way of giving of yourself to another.

I will discuss some biblical and practical truths about sexuality to optimize sexual intimacy between a husband and wife as well as sexual issues that can limit a couple's sexual connectedness in week three.

Day 7

THREE DAILY EXERCISES

Pray together? _____ Yes _____ No

What did you pray?

_____

_____

_____

Feelings exercise? _____ Yes _____ No

He shared   _____

                    (feeling #1)

     and   _____

                    (feeling #2)

She shared   _____

                    (feeling #1)

     and   _____

                    (feeling #2)

Praise/nurture together? _____ Yes _____ No

He shared   _____

              (praise #1)

She shared   _____

              (praise #1)

He shared   _____

              (praise #2)

She shared   _____

              (praise #2)

Week 1

PROGRESS NOTES

Record your progress for the week on your spiritual exercise of prayer.

Husband: 1   2   3   4   5   6   7

Wife: 1   2   3   4   5   6   7

Record your progress on your feelings exercise.

Husband: 1   2   3   4   5   6   7

Wife: 1   2   3   4   5   6   7

Record your progress on the praise and nurturing exercise.

Husband: 1   2   3   4   5   6   7

Wife: 1   2   3   4   5   6   7

Additional constructive thoughts, comments, or observations

_____

_____

_____

_____

WEEK 2

EMOTIONAL MAKEOVER

Day 8

IS YOUR MARRIAGE BASED ON EMOTION?

Like a city whose walls are broken down is a man who lacks self-control.
—PROVERBS 25:28

A POWERFUL DYNAMIC THAT sabotages intimacy is what I call the "emotion-based marriage." Chaos, lack of follow-through, and inconsistency characterize these marriages.

There are two types of emotion-based marriages. The first is what I call the "benign" form. The second form is "malignant" yet treatable. I encourage you to walk through this section—even if it doesn't apply to you—because you will probably know marriages that function this way and can better understand why.

THE BENIGN MARRIAGE

I know a couple from another state who were both saved as adults. The husband is a professional in his career. They have two children and are very active at church. Their house is always in a state of total chaos—clothes strewn everywhere, dishes in the sink, beds unmade. They stay so busy that regular fellowship with them is difficult. They have no time for systems of intimacy such as prayer, sharing feelings, dating, and

59

finances, so everything is always in a state of flux. They seem always to be going around in the same circles, never really gaining momentum in their relationship.

This is the benign form of an emotion-based marriage system. In this system no one is really intentionally trying to be difficult or to harm the other. They simply can't seem to "get it together."

A couple such as this one may try therapy, but they continue doing their homework for only a short period of time. When asked why they didn't follow through with it, they rarely can come up with any tangible reasons.

The entire notion of practiced consistency or principle-based thinking eludes them totally. Their decisions are made emotionally, and their schedule constantly changes simply because they felt like doing something else instead. At that point they are unable to remember previous commitments and totally miss events they had planned.

Such couples are often pleasant and fun to be with, at least when things are going well with them. They simply have no structure in their lives.

Progress is slow in a marriage with the benign form of an emotion-based marriage. Trying to get a commitment from this couple simply to pray together is difficult. When they get into a system for a few weeks, they feel closer than ever, but they eventually stop, and then their relationship deteriorates again.

The reason for the marital deterioration is that this couple's emotions dominate the decision-making process. If they feel like doing something, they do, and if they don't (even if it is biblical), then they just don't do it. Period! The sixties' culture raised a generation that bought into a lifestyle of "if it feels good, do it." The concept of restraint, principles, and accountability are not factored into their decision-making process.

This type of an emotion-based marriage system wreaks havoc on intimacy, since intimacy building is much more than just making up after big fights. Intimacy for a lifetime requires more than just fleeting moments of discipline. Intimacy is the result of a disciplined lifestyle. Intimacy is relational wealth that accumulates over a lifetime of invested, consistent behavior. Intimacy, like wealth, doesn't just happen. It is painstakingly planned, worked for, and achieved along the way while two hearts are consistently being open and available to each other.

A couple within an emotion-based system will honestly find it difficult to change. Even the benign structure meets disciplined changes with great resistance. The chaos within this system gives the couple great distraction from the lack of structure in the relationship. Crises appear from out of nowhere, such as when one or both of the partner's needs are not being met, and stress appears in the marriage. Plans for the future are avoided, and a flat tire just happens. With each crisis, the cycle of the emotion-based marriage starts over once again.

THE MALIGNANT MARRIAGE

The malignant form of the emotion-based marriage system is willful. In this marriage not only are the husband and/or wife making their decisions based upon their emotions, but they also refuse instruction, information, or connection from anyone in authority, including God. They are bent on doing what they want regardless of the results. If one person wants to neglect his or her spouse for days or weeks to punish that person, he or she will. If they want to make a financial decision regardless of the consequences, they will.

This selfishness at the cost of others becomes toxic. The intimacy within the relationship is inconsistent and even volatile. Anger or silence is used to control the spouse and other family members as well. You know you're in a marriage like this when the major goal of the family is to keep this spouse happy.

The malignant form of an emotion-based marriage can sometimes be a result of several undiagnosed forms of emotional disorders. Addictions may be present, such as addictions to work, alcohol, drugs, or sex. Professional help may need to be obtained for these issues to be resolved.

In some relationships one spouse may have a mood disorder called *bipolar disorder* (also known as manic-depressive disorder). On some days this husband or wife will be happy, motivated, clear thinking, and fun to be around. Then, out of the blue will come one to three days of depression, moodiness, and irritable behavior. Now no one in the family can do anything right, and soon everyone starts to think, "Why even bother?" After a couple of days of gloom, the bipolar person cycles back and becomes cheerful. This disorder can keep an emotion-based marriage in a particularly toxic state.

If an emotion-based system is in the malignant form and addictions or mood disorders are not present, the problem may simply be a heart attitude that suggests, "I do what I want, and if you don't like it, leave." Often those with this heart attitude reject their spouse's appeal for intimacy by saying their partner is just needy or weak. The one seeking intimacy feels as though his or her spouse can't or won't let them in.

If you're reading this section, and it feels as if you are in a malignant or toxic emotion-based marriage system, you probably will need further professional help to get to the other side of intimacy with your spouse. The emotion-based marriage system can be a major roadblock to intimacy. Real problems need to be addressed. If you are in this situation, you will benefit greatly by reading days 11 and 12 of this week. Do as many of the structured exercises in this guide as you can. If you feel that you need professional help, ask your pastor for a referral.

Complete the questions below to help determine if you are in an emotionally based marriage.

AN EMOTION-BASED MARRIAGE?

☐ Yes ☐ No 1. Does your marriage and family life feel chaotic most of the time?

☐ Yes ☐ No 2. Does it feel as if there is no consistent spiritual and emotional connection with your spouse?

☐ Yes ☐ No 3. Does money get spent regularly without anyone really knowing where it went?

☐ Yes ☐ No 4. Does it appear that you are not working toward long-term retirement plans?

☐ Yes ☐ No 5. Does it seem that some things never get done?

☐ Yes ☐ No 6. Does the way decisions get made within the marriage seem unclear?

If you answered yes to most of the previous questions, your marriage may be built on an emotion-based marriage system. Tomorrow I will tell you the best ways to move from a marriage run by emotions to a marriage that is steadied by principles.

Day 8

THREE DAILY EXERCISES

Pray together? _____ Yes _____ No

What did you pray?

_____

_____

_____

Feelings exercise? _____ Yes _____ No

He shared   _____

                (feeling #1)

     and   _____

                (feeling #2)

She shared   _____

                (feeling #1)

     and   _____

                (feeling #2)

Praise/nurture together? _____ Yes _____ No

He shared _____

          (praise #1)

She shared _____

          (praise #1)

He shared _____

          (praise #2)

She shared _____

          (praise #2)

Day 9

SOLUTIONS FOR AN EMOTION-BASED MARRIAGE

*Whoever has no rule over his own spirit is like
a city broken down, without walls.*
—Proverbs 25:28, NKJV

THE OPPOSITE OF an emotion-based marriage system is a principle-based relationship. Over time intimacy flourishes in this type of marriage. Principles, both biblical and practical, guide the decision-making process. A personality doesn't dominate, nor do the desires of one person in the marriage.

The relationship has structure and boundaries with consequences so that both spouses can be themselves without hurting the other. These couples make decisions based upon whether or not something is right or if it was already agreed upon, not just because of how they feel at a particular moment in time.

A couple that lives within the parameters of a principle-based relationship has the highest chance of getting and maintaining lifelong intimacy that benefits both spouses. They don't tithe simply when they feel like it—they decide to tithe and do it. They don't pray together coincidentally, accidentally, or occasionally—they pray intentionally and regularly.

This couple works together to solve problems, and they don't just serve their own emotions. If they don't feel like doing something they have committed to doing, they stick with it through the initial stages of discomfort because they made a commitment.

If your relationship is more emotionally based than you would like, don't be discouraged. As we walk through the practical applications in this guide, any couple can make great progress.

WHEN ONE PARTNER NEEDS TO GROW

Emotional systems can result from one or both spouses who are behaving as children or adolescents rather than adults in an area of life. It's possible to be an adult in one area of life but an adolescent or a child in another. The imbalance created by this dynamic can cause an emotion-based marriage system.

Many people have married individuals who can carry the areas in themselves in which they are uncomfortable. The problem is that these issues are never discussed, but instead they are allowed to evolve into emotional systems that create roadblocks to intimacy.

When both spouses do not function as adults within their relationship, they will be robbed of intimacy. Many couples create emotion-based marriage systems without even knowing it. Use the following chart for self-improvement. You may notice the undeveloped areas in your spouse, but that is not the purpose for the chart.

You *cannot* change your spouse. Therefore, unless you use this information for individual prayer, in a loving and therapeutic manner, or in an agreed-upon conversation with your spouse, it will be unproductive. Please don't use this information to attack, shame, or otherwise injure the soul of your spouse. Use it only to improve *yourself*.

DEVELOPING YOUR RELATIONSHIP

Area	Child	Adolescent	Adult
Spiritual	Refuses to feed themselves by reading the Bible Wants others to feed them by attending church only Prayer is not really initiated on a regular basis Likes it if "you" pray. States that the Bible is too difficult to understand Doesn't feel convicted of sin on any regular basis	Feeds themselves Their interpretation of Scripture is "the" interpretation Prays but is inconsistent Will pray together "if you make them" Struggles with balancing biblical truths Convicted of sin but has struggles with authority issues	Feeds themselves regularly Feeds others in their life by character and word Prayer is consistent and desired Desires to pray with you anytime Convicted of even minor sin regularly
Social	Does not initiate in relationships Only responds to those who want to initiate toward them Can't seem to find a person or group to connect to Most of their friends do all the work in their relationship	Will initiate in relationship if it serves a purpose Relationship based on activities Tends to have a rotating best friend Does some initiating in the relationship to set up activities	Can initiate a relationship with those just because, with no need to serve a purpose Can create time just for relating, not requiring an activity Can have long-term friendships Accepts the seasons of friendships Tends to initiate equally in a relationship

Area	Child	Adolescent	Adult
Financial	Refuses to have anything to do with money issues Money things are just overwhelming Has a naïve status toward taxes and retirement As long as their needs are met there is no real need to talk about it Doesn't write checks or know the bills	Financially selfish Thinks in short term, materialistic tendencies Toys are more important than future planning What they are, what the family looks like (house, cars, clothes) is really important Credit card debt is very common Will tithe when convenient	Money has spiritual meaning Long-term planning is part of their thought process Short-term sacrifice is honorable for long-term gain Tithing is consistent
Sexual	Does not accept or see themselves as sexual Will not initiate sex Talking about sex is always inappropriate	Sex is for them mostly Unaware of spouse's sexual needs Angry when their needs don't get met Sex conversations seem to feel cheap and not about intimacy	Accepts themselves sexually Accepts the sexuality of their spouse Has intimacy during sexuality Maintains sexual integrity
Feelings	Doesn't know what you're talking about Becomes confused when emotions are addressed Feels you're asking too much of them to do feelings work	Has feelings but a limited ability to communicate them Has periods of emotional constipation, then blows up or gets silent Really more concerned about their feelings and not yours	Has feelings and the ability to communicate them Can be emotionally safe and keep confidences Values and hears the feelings of their spouses
Fun	Can have some fun if others plan for it Loves to be invited but has little fun on their own Often unable to be silly at appropriate times	Fun is what life is about Keeps self preoccupied by several hobbies Selfish with their time off and vacation Most of their friends revolve around hobbies	Can plan fun for self and others Realizes the importance of fun in balance Will take some time for self but balances it with their spouse

In the columns in the next chart, indicate where you believe you may fit in the various areas. It is appropriate to do this portion on a separate sheet of paper if you feel more comfortable. Score yourself individually. I know you can't help but score your spouse, so if you do, don't tell them. They may disagree.

INDIVIDUAL EMOTIONAL SYSTEM DEVELOPMENT

Husband (check where appropriate)

Area	Child	Adolescent	Adult
Spiritual			
Social			
Financial			
Sexual			
Feelings			
Fun			

Wife (check where appropriate)

Area	Child	Adolescent	Adult
Spiritual			
Social			
Financial			
Sexual			
Feelings			
Fun			

Before you go further, if you agreed with your spouse to disclose your analysis to each other, talk over your responses now. If both have not agreed to do this, then please don't force the matter until you do agree.

These issues are emotionally based and often are hot buttons within a marriage. Resolving these issues will require work as individuals, not as a couple. Your work together as a couple begins when you move beyond these issues and can discuss them and see the impact that your personal development or lack of development is making on the marriage.

Discussing your emotional systems can move you toward creating the structural system that you both choose.

When you both want to discuss these emotional systems with each other, you can. Check off the area of self-report that you feel ready to discuss with your spouse.

SELF-REPORTED AREAS

Area	Spouse	Child	Adolescent	Adult
Spiritual	Him			
	Her			
Social	Him			
	Her			
Financial	Him			
	Her			
Sexual	Him			
	Her			
Feelings	Him			
	Her			
Fun	Him			
	Her			

What were the apparent areas that each of you needs to address to have fewer roadblocks to future intimacy?

His Areas	Her Areas
1.	1.
2.	2.
3.	3.
4.	4.

As a couple, what areas seem to be impacted by the individual emotional systems?

Yes	No	Areas
		Spiritual
		Social
		Financial
		Sexual
		Feelings
		Fun

Better to Make a Plan Than to Make Excuses

As an adult, you are responsible for yourself. You alone can decide to become more mature in these areas. Only you can stop your individual emotional systems from creating emotion-based marriage systems in your relationship.

You're not alone. You have the love, knowledge, and support of counselors and of Christ and His Word, the Bible. You have a spouse who loves you. You can choose to take these roadblocks out of your way.

I realize that it's difficult work. I have had to grow up in every area that we have covered. It was hard work, and maintaining what you gain can be just as difficult at times. But in my life I have found that it is better to make a plan than to make excuses. I pray God's speed and wisdom for you as you love yourself and your marriage enough to strengthen the areas where you are lacking.

Day 9

THREE DAILY EXERCISES

Pray together? _____ Yes _____ No

What did you pray?

_____

_____

_____

Feelings exercise? _____ Yes _____ No

He shared   _____

            (feeling #1)

    and   _____

            (feeling #2)

She shared   _____

            (feeling #1)

    and   _____

            (feeling #2)

Praise/nurture together? _____ Yes _____ No

He shared _____

(praise #1)

She shared _____

(praise #1)

He shared _____

(praise #2)

She shared _____

(praise #2)

Day 10

OVERCOMING EMOTIONAL
CONSTIPATION

We will no longer be infants.... Instead, speaking the truth in love, we
will in all things grow up into him who is the Head, that is, Christ.
—EPHESIANS 4:14–15

EMOTIONS ARE POWERFUL. If they have only three outlets, as mine did, it can cause "emotional constipation." Emotional constipation is when a person has many more feelings than he or she has the skills to express or identify. This constipation will show itself differently in various people. Some fly into rages, while others pout or stop talking to their spouse for days at a time. Regardless of how this constipation manifests, it never moves a couple toward intimacy.

This constipation can be a roadblock to connecting emotionally. Suppose I am in a marriage with only three feeling options: angry, really angry, and "other." Now suppose that I also marry someone with only three emotional options: angry, really angry, and "other."

Now the fun begins. Let's suppose that one day I really feel rejected, and I have to decide how to express my "rejected" feeling. After thinking a little bit, I may decide that angry would be the best "door" to pick for my rejected feeling. My wife, on the other hand, may feel alone and unimportant, but she chooses the "other" door to express these feelings.

When I come home from work, I'm showing anger (door number one). She is expressing door number three ("other") for her feelings of being alone and unimportant. Now we are off to the races.

This is the emotionally constipated way of communicating. We are unable to identify our real emotions, but we are still trying to get our points across. If your relationship has ever been there, you know that it can take hours or days to sort through the confusion.

If you don't have the ability to identify your own emotions, then how can you share them with your spouse? You can miss the blessing of sharing yourself emotionally with your spouse, not because of spitefulness but simply because you honestly don't know how.

Again, this goes back to a skill that was never developed. The good thing about this problem is that the solution is simply a skill issue that can be learned! It took a little time for me to learn my own feelings, but once I did, our miscommunication problem happened much less. I truly can't remember when we had our last big emotionally constipated disagreement.

Once you complete this skill-building program, you will be able to better identify your own feelings and effectively share them with your spouse. You will truly be amazed at how emotionally connected you can become in a very short period of time when you are faithful to do these daily exercises. You will find that overcoming emotional constipation will dramatically help you to build and maintain connectedness or emotional intimacy.

We all need emotional connectedness—and I do mean *need*! Weary is the soul that has no one with whom to share. We all need someone who will hear us. Being able to share yourself and to be heard are basic, legitimate God-given needs. Your need for emotional connectedness is no less legitimate than your need for food and water. When you genuinely accept this as truth, you will be able to take responsibility to make sure that your own needs and your spouse's needs are met on a regular basis.

I remember when Tom and Kathryn, an older couple from the Northeast, attended their first counseling session with me. Tom had been an engineer for more than thirty-five years. He was a godly man who loved the Lord, his wife, and his children. If you knew Tom, you would probably agree that he was a pragmatic, smart man who knew his Bible well. After all the children grew up and left home, Kathryn decided they needed to come for counseling. She was not feeling nurtured. She might have phrased it like this: "I feel dry inside. I don't really know what is going on inside of Tom. He doesn't talk to me."

I knew exactly what Kathryn was trying to communicate. Tom did not know how to share his feelings with her. Now, in Tom's defense, he grew up on a farm in Missouri as one of seven children, five of whom were boys. He grew up poor and worked hard. His family didn't discuss their feelings, just what farm work needed to get done. His parents were good people, but they left Tom with no emotional skills.

Tom went off to college, worked his way through an engineering program, and enjoyed a successful career at an engineering firm. Unlike psychology, the field of engineering never requires you to discuss your feelings or to develop emotionally during the learning process. In Tom's career, feelings were irrelevant.

On the other hand, Kathryn had grown up freely expressing her feelings. As one of three sisters, she talked about her feelings all the time. When Kathryn married Tom, she was full of love and devotion. She felt alone in the earlier years of the marriage until she had her children. Then she threw herself into raising her son and daughter. Tom provided well, and they functioned well together as parents and church members.

Now that the children were gone, Kathryn was again feeling as disconnected and alone as she felt in the earlier years of her marriage. She couldn't face looking at twenty-five or more years of feeling alone in marriage again.

Tom loved Kathryn, but he didn't understand what she needed. I tried to help. "Kathryn is like the engine of your car, Tom," I told him. "You wouldn't let your engine go without oil, would you?"

Tom said no. A good engineer couldn't imagine such a thing.

"If you let your oil go, eventually your engine will make all kinds of unpleasant, strange-sounding noises. Eventually it would just freeze up and stop working, wouldn't it?"

Tom said, "Of course."

I explained that his wife needed to have emotional oil in her engine to run properly—the way God intended. "Tom," I continued, "if you don't give her the oil, eventually funny noises will happen, and one day the engine will just quit."

After equipping Tom with the skills he needed to connect emotionally with his wife, they were well on their way to emotional intimacy. Tom realized that not only did his wife have emotional needs, but he also needed to connect and share. What a positive difference connectedness made in Tom and Kathryn's lives.

HONORING EMOTIONS

To acquire the skills necessary for emotional intimacy, we must shift the way we think about emotions. We must learn to honor them. By honoring emotions, you assert that they are a real, valuable, precious part of the person you love. These feelings are an essential part of your spouse's being.

As human beings we can think and behave differently than we feel, but we can't feel differently than we feel. Here is an illustration to help you understand this better. Think of a person at work whose behavior irritates you deep down inside. When you're with him, you act and behave appropriately so that no one knows how you really feel. If that person were to come into your office and ask you to tell him honestly how you "feel" about him, you would be honest and share the truth. At that point he would know about you and your feelings toward him.

I say this to illustrate that our emotions are who we are. If I feel tired, then I am tired. That is who I am at that microsecond of time. Now here is the tricky part. Feelings may be real and a real part of who I am, but they are not necessarily truth, and they change constantly.

Early in my career as a therapist I authored my first book, and things seemed to be going well for me at the time. We were in the process of shooting two large national television shows per month, and financially everything was solid. One night I remember crawling into bed, and as is our custom, we began sharing our feelings.

"I want to share a feeling that makes no sense," I told Lisa. "It isn't true, but for whatever unknown reason, I am feeling it today. I feel unsuccessful."

Lisa honored my feelings as a feeling and didn't try to fix it, change it, or rationalize it away.

The unsuccessful feeling was just a feeling—nothing more, nothing less. All of our feelings change constantly. Most of us can barely recall even a few of the feelings we had a week ago.

Learning to honor your spouse's feelings places you in a precarious balance. When you hear your spouse's feelings, you must honor them immediately. They are precious offerings to you at the time of sharing. However, you must resist the temptation to change, alter, or rationalize away what he or she may be feeling at the moment. Our spouses will not feel any one particular feeling forever. Feelings change, and being honored and heard are very important.

Men in particular have more difficulty just sharing feelings instead of trying to solve problems. But as you grow in the skill of sharing, hearing, and honoring the feelings of your spouse, the quality of emotional intimacy soars. When I feel safe and honored as I share my feelings, I am more likely to keep sharing them with others as well.

When you decide to honor your spouse emotionally on a regular basis, you will begin to see your spouse as the best person on the earth to be with. I know that I can share any feelings with Lisa and still feel accepted by her. When she honors my emotions, it makes me feel special, important, and loved by my wife.

Your spouse and his or her emotions are ever changing. Honoring your spouse's emotions without feeling the need to fix them or fix the situation will produce enormous positive fruit in your relationship. So make a decision to travel through the next thirty days together honoring your spouse's emotions and cherishing the person he or she is on the inside.

Day 10

THREE DAILY EXERCISES

Pray together? _____ Yes _____ No

What did you pray?

_____

_____

Feelings exercise? _____ Yes _____ No

He shared _____

              (feeling #1)

    and _____

              (feeling #2)

She shared _____

              (feeling #1)

    and _____

              (feeling #2)

Praise/nurture together? _____ Yes _____ No

He shared _____

(praise #1)

She shared _____

(praise #1)

He shared _____

(praise #2)

She shared _____

(praise #2)

Day 11

THE ANGER ENEMY

See to it that no one misses the grace of God and that no
bitter root grows up to cause trouble and defile many.
—HEBREWS 12:15

SMALL INFRACTIONS CAUSED by a couple's sins and unresolved conflicts during the course of a marriage create roadblocks to intimacy. The onslaught of trauma experienced by other couples causes deep, destructive rifts.

Neglect and abuse, which accompany addictions to alcohol, drugs, sex, food, and work, can seriously damage the spouse married to an addict. Lies, empty promises, and the roller-coaster rides that typify these addictive marriages create truly indescribable pain.

The scarring of physical and mental abuse causes more than just a buildup of painful events—it often causes legitimate rage. The effects of sexual infidelity, rape, and child abuse will most certainly traumatize any marriage, even those appearing to be very religious. Although such things "should" not happen in Christian marriages, I know they do.

On the other side of abuse is neglect. Neglect is more common in Christian marriages seeking help. Prayerlessness in a Christian couple's relationship is definitely a form of neglect. I cannot tell you how many women have come to my office over the years complaining about the lack of connection with their spouse.

Refusing to share your heart, coupled with an absence of prayer and praise over the decades, will create a silent anger, an internal rage within your spouse. This serious roadblock stunts the growth of trust and intimacy and can create real problems down the road for the couple who remains together.

Adulterous situations throw a spouse into a traumatic situation that he or she must then attempt to handle. To expect the spouse in an adulterous situation to simply move on and put the matter behind him or her minimizes the trauma. Adultery affects the spirit, soul, and body, creating deep wounds in one or both spouses.

This type of wounding requires time to heal. Saying "I am sorry" will not make the pain disappear. I have personally experienced several traumas throughout my life prior to my marriage. My soul was wounded before I became married, so I am personally aware of how trauma affects the ability to be intimate.

In many relationships trust has been broken, decency has been violated, and healing must take place in the soul of the wounded spouse. This individual is thrust into a paradoxical situation. Unfortunately the person whom he or she loves the most may also be the one with whom he is most angry, and for good reason. This is an internal controversy that says "I love you" and "I'd like to pound you!" all at the same time.

If you are a wounded spouse, the perpetrator is responsible for your feelings. Yet the responsibility to heal is yours. If I happened to walk outside, and a sniper randomly shot me, I would be responsible to heal and repair from the damage of this event. I'm the one who would have to do what the doctor or physical therapist advised if I wanted to be restored. The following story will help make my point more clear.

Jake and Fran are a couple who had been married for over forty years. He drank some, and on a couple of occasions he physically abused Fran and sexually forced himself on her, which is rape. They had children, and Jake became a workaholic. As a salesman he traveled three to five days a week, abandoning his wife with the children.

While Jake was traveling, he had several affairs that Fran found out about much later. Jake had a born-again experience after their last child left home to attend college. He changed completely and began to live a genuine Christian life of integrity. Jake stopped traveling, and he and Fran began working at improving their marriage. Although both were Christians (she had prayed for him for years), they struggled with intimacy.

Jake protested, "She just won't forgive me for the past. I am a new creature now!" He cited 2 Corinthians 5:17, "Therefore, if anyone is in Christ, he is a new creation; the old has gone, the new has come!"

Fran continued to feel stuck in her past feelings. She verbalized her forgiveness, but she still felt that she couldn't totally trust him and didn't appear to want to connect intimately with him.

Fran's past wounding needed to be healed before intimacy could take place. Such pain goes far deeper than merely seeking forgiveness for past offenses. This spouse needed support, not criticism, to get through this.

Alan and Barb were another wounded couple that needed healing.

Alan and Barb are a Christian couple with a middle-class income. In the earlier days of the marriage, Barb was an out-of-control shopper. Today she says, "I was definitely a shop-a-holic! I didn't even need the stuff that I would buy. I just shopped to try not to feel anything and to make myself feel better."

Barb constantly berated Alan, who was in his twenties at the time, because they couldn't afford the bigger car, a larger house, and couldn't live like some of their forty-year-old friends who traveled all the time. She would shame him and was constantly critical of him. She conveyed the messages "You're not good enough," "You'll never measure up," and "I'm not proud of you."

Alan really took these messages to heart! He spent more than fifteen years climbing the ladder to success and rarely received praise for all of his hard work. Alan and Barb were both Christians during their entire marriage. Years later, Barb was convicted about her spending behavior, which she felt was an addiction. She went to therapy and group counseling and had not relapsed with shopping for a long time.

From the outside everything looked good. But on the inside Alan was distant, continued to mistrust his wife, and did not feel loved by her. He stated he has tried many times to forgive her, but he still battles with outbursts of rage during which he will say regretful things to her and stay distant from her for days.

Alan had hidden anger. The wounds his wife inflicted on him had built up inside over years. He was understandably angry about the painful events that took place in his marriage. He loved his wife, but he didn't feel as if he really liked her. Alan didn't want to deal with the trust issues he had involving Barb. He felt sorry following blowout arguments and truly wanted to know his wife the way Christ wants him to. Nevertheless, he kept hitting what he called "the wall." "I just can't let her in," he said in our counseling sessions.

Is Alan truly not forgiving Barb, or is he trying to punish her? I don't believe he is doing either. Alan experienced trauma throughout his years of marriage because of his wife's behavior and has internalized legitimate anger. This hidden anger (hidden even to Alan) is now a roadblock to intimacy with his wife, whom deep down he truly loves.

Anger is a familiar problem in many marriages, and it must be taken seriously as you strive to be intimate with your spouse. Only when wounds inside a relationship are identified and addressed biblically can healing begin to take place. When wounds are healed, a totally new level of intimacy can follow.

A spouse may have entered into a marriage with wounds from the past, and new wounds may occur during the marriage. In other marriages, both partners may be wounded. For example, when a husband and wife survive the same car accident, each may have his own physical bruises, bandages, and pain. As they sleep together in the same bed, when one turns over, the other cries out in pain. Emotional pain responds the same.

Silent anger about your wounds can block intimacy, even when you long for it in your marriage. You can be healed from inner pain, regardless of the source. Once you identify the roadblock and take responsibility for your own healing, you can begin to move forward once again.

I have seen many courageous men and women identify and receive healing from the wounds that their spouses have inflicted on them. All forms of abuse, neglect, infidelity, addictions, and shame can be successfully overcome with the desire to do so.

Regardless of the past, healing can take place. It requires work and patience, but the results are nothing short of marvelous. As a Christian counselor, I have witnessed the healing of deep wounds and broken marriages. I have watched as couples reclaimed intimacy and once again became vibrant and sexually passionate. We serve a great God, and as a colaborer with Him, all things are possible.

Tomorrow's exercise, called "cleansing the temple," is designed to help you get free from past hurts and wounds. I have witnessed tremendous grace come into the hearts of those who follow this exercise.

Day 11

THREE DAILY EXERCISES

Pray together? _____ Yes _____ No

What did you pray?

_____

_____

_____

Feelings exercise? _____ Yes _____ No

He shared _____

           (feeling #1)

   and _____

           (feeling #2)

She shared _____

           (feeling #1)

   and _____

           (feeling #2)

Praise/nurture together? _____ Yes _____ No

He shared   _____

                 (praise #1)

She shared   _____

                 (praise #1)

He shared   _____

                 (praise #2)

She shared   _____

                 (praise #2)

Day 12

CLEANSING THE TEMPLE

Don't you know that you yourselves are God's temple and that
God's Spirit lives in you? If anyone destroys God's temple, God will
destroy him; for God's temple is sacred, and you are that temple.
—1 CORINTHIANS 3:16–17

THIS EXERCISE CAN remove a lot of the pain that you may carry in your soul. This pain may be from your family of origin and caused by neglect, abuse, or abandonment. It may be from childhood sexual abuse or rape. Some pain carried in your soul is from your spouse. In some marriages, spouses traumatize one another or deprive one another to such a degree that their anger seems overwhelming.

Anger can build up in your soul until the size of your wound makes intimacy extremely difficult. Even though you did not cause the wounds, you are now responsible to receive healing for them. Similar to walking outside and getting shot by a sniper, you are 100 percent responsible to receive healing from your wounds, even though the sniper is 100 percent responsible for causing the wound.

In our culture, victim status is power. This power is wielded through manipulation to make other people pay, or it is used as an excuse to abdicate responsibility for yourself or the direction of your life.

This cleansing the temple exercise is based on the biblical account of

Jesus cleansing the temple. The account of this is found in each Gospel. (See Matthew 21; Mark 11; Luke 19; and John 2.) Let's review the four major principles from John 2:13–22, and then we will walk through the practical application.

BIBLICAL PRINCIPLES

Principle 1—Jesus knew the temple needed to be cleansed.

In the first three accounts of Jesus cleansing the temple, the *temple* refers to a physical building in Jerusalem. But in John's account Jesus refers to His body (John 2:18–21). Jesus was changing the dwelling place of God from the physical temple to the temple of a human being. Paul develops this thought a little later when he records that Christian believers are God's temple (1 Cor. 3:16–17).

God's plan all along was to dwell inside of us. We are His holy temple. This being true, temples can become defiled through many avenues, including manipulation, abuse, and neglect from others. When we get defiled through life, our temple gets defiled also and needs to get cleaned out as well.

It's interesting that Jesus, the owner of the temple, was the one who took full responsibility to clean His own temple. He could have made the perpetrators in the story, who were the moneychangers and sellers of doves, clean up their own mess, but He didn't. He cleansed the temple Himself.

We are the possessors of our temple. If our temples get defiled through the abuse of others, we are the ones who must clean it up. The person who hurt us may say he is sorry, but that doesn't get rid of the muck or defilement that has been placed inside our souls. We still must clean up the mess.

By cleaning His own temple, Jesus sends a clear message to us: we are responsible to clean our own temples as well.

Principle 2—Jesus identified the sin that caused the defilement.

Jesus made it very clear to them why He was cleansing the temple (John 2:16). They were taking something holy and misusing it to profit themselves. Most of the people who have hurt you have no concept of your holiness or preciousness. You have felt used or abused during the incidents in which you were wounded. You will need to identify the sin or damage that has been done to you by those who have defiled your temple.

Principle 3—Jesus focused His anger at the injustice.

Jesus wasn't merely having a bad day. This was an act of His will. It was a well-thought-out act of obedience. This is an important point to understand, because it will take an act of your will to clean your temple.

Jesus intentionally planned to upset the normal course of events in His temple. John's account says, "He found men selling cattle, sheep and doves, and others sitting at tables exchanging money. So he made a whip out of cords" (John 2:14–15). This passage gives us the sense that Jesus was looking around and witnessing the peoples' mistreatment of His holy temple. Then, in verse 15, He gets a bunch of cords and takes the time to make a whip. He had already decided to use that whip when He entered His temple to cleanse it.

As we proceed with this exercise, you will need to make choices to prioritize your time to prepare for cleansing your temple. Those who go about this intentionally and purposefully have received great breakthroughs in their lives.

Principle 4—The temple was restored to its original order.

Why do we just treat trauma cognitively and expect people to heal? If the trauma affects all three dimensions of a person, doesn't it make sense that the healing of trauma involves all three aspects—spirit, soul, and body—as well?

I share the same logic with you. People may have hurt you significantly. You may have presumed to forgive them, and you have done so. Nevertheless, the bullet is still inside. The muck and defilement are still surrounding it. That doesn't necessarily mean you didn't forgive them—it just means that you haven't cleansed your temple yet.

My experience with cleansing the temple has been nothing short of miraculous. Sexual abuse survivors heal very quickly after this exercise. Women who have been sexually betrayed by their husbands move through the stages of grief and forgiveness much more quickly than those who refuse to cleanse their temple.

The "Cleanse the Temple" Exercise

1. Write an anger letter.

The first step in the cleansing of your temple is to write an anger letter to the person who has hurt you, but don't send it. Imagine this person in the room with you, but he or she is unable to talk or move. You can say whatever you need to say to him or her in this letter. This is not a letter to suppress your feelings but rather to vent all the thoughts and feelings of hate, disgust, and anguish that have been robbing your soul. Neither is this an "I forgive you" letter. That will come later. This is the place where you rid yourself of the anger that has been a part of your soul.

2. Get warmed up.

In Jesus's situation He made a whip for Himself. I don't recommend whips, but a padded baseball bat or tennis racket could be helpful. First, warm up your body. Take your bat and hit a mattress or pillow with small hits. Then use medium, large, and extra large hits. Do this three times. Warm up your voice as well. Shout no each time you hit the pillow. Use small, medium, large, and extra large nos with your voice. This may feel awkward, but removing this buildup of pain from your soul and spirit feels almost like having a baby. That is why it's important to be warmed up physically.

While you're warming up, make sure you are home alone. Disconnect the phone so that you are not disturbed.

Note: Before doing this, if you have a heart condition or other medical condition that warrants talking to your medical doctor first, please do so.

3. Read your letter aloud.

After your physical warm-up, take the letter you wrote to your offender and read it aloud. If your offender's name is Toby, then you would read as follows: "Toby, how could you have done this to me? I trusted you!"

Of course, Toby is nowhere around. You certainly don't need to do this with him or her around. You are simply in a room alone, just reading the letter aloud.

4. Engage your anger physically and verbally.

After reading your letter, pick up your bat. Hit the bed or pillow and symbolically let "Toby" have it. You can yell, scream, and cry, but release the infection that has been robbing you. You can symbolically tell him that his secrets are not controlling you any more. He was to blame! You have no limits as to what you can say to your offender. For once, let go of all the emotional control that is keeping this wound infected. Let it out!

This can last from fifteen minutes to an hour. Your body will let you know when you have completely put this behind you—spiritually, emotionally, and physically.

Someone has given you something toxic, and you have been unhealthy ever since. After you remove it from you, you will feel so much better. You're worth getting it all out!

Comments

When you do this cleansing exercise, only work on one offender at a time. If three different people have offended you, then you will need to complete three different sessions. *Do not* try to go through this exercise just once for all the different people who have offended you. Each "bullet" needs to be taken out separately.

Start with the least painful trauma and work your way up to the larger offenses. In this way you will get better skilled at the exercise and will know what to expect.

Remember, you're cleansing your temple so that during these thirty days you can experience the absolute best intimacy possible. Carrying pain inside causes you to protect yourself from being hurt. In the process, you also protect yourself from being intimate.

As you read through this exercise together, you don't need discuss with each other to whom you will write a letter. But do take a moment to discuss when you can be home alone to do your own cleansing the temple exercise. By making a commitment to set aside the time to do this work, you will be much more likely to follow through with it. The sooner this takes place, the better it will be for both of you.

Day 12

THREE DAILY EXERCISES

Pray together? _____ Yes _____ No

What did you pray?

_____

_____

_____

Feelings exercise? _____ Yes _____ No

He shared _____

               (feeling #1)

    and _____

               (feeling #2)

She shared _____

               (feeling #1)

    and _____

               (feeling #2)

Praise/nurture together? _____ Yes _____ No

He shared   _____

               (praise #1)

She shared   _____

               (praise #1)

He shared   _____

               (praise #2)

She shared   _____

               (praise #2)

Day 13

FORGIVENESS

*Then Peter came to Jesus and asked, "Lord, how many times shall I
forgive my brother when he sins against me? Up to seven times?" Jesus
answered, "I tell you, not seven times, but seventy-seven times."*

—MATTHEW 18:21–22

THIS NEXT STAGE of healing is only for those who have already
cleansed their temple. It should be completed about five days
after you have completed the anger work of cleansing the temple
regarding a particular offender.

Five days or more after finishing your anger work, you should be
feeling much better. It is similar to how you feel after getting over a
cold. You can feel that the junk in your lungs is gone, and you can
breathe more clearly and easily now.

Several clients have shared that after doing the cleansing the temple
exercise with a focus on their mom or dad, the next time they visited their
parents they didn't get all knotted up or tight inside. After completing
this exercise, most people can reenter the relationship without pain.

The next step to healing is forgiveness. I am not suggesting that you
look up your violators and tell them you forgive them. Rather, I am
talking about doing another therapeutic exercise so you can see how far
along in the process of forgiveness you really are with this person.

97

The following exercise is very effective, and most are able to choose to forgive their offenders. The Bible is full of teachings on forgiveness. It might be helpful to get a concordance and look up all of the verses listed under the word *forgiveness*. Start with Matthew 6:14–15:

> For if you forgive men when they sin against you, your heavenly Father will also forgive you. But if you do not forgive men their sins, your Father will not forgive your sins.

Work your way through the entire New Testament regarding forgiveness. I realize that for some individuals, healing and cleansing will need to come first before they are truly able to forgive from their heart. For a whole book on the subject of forgiveness, I would recommend *The Bait of Satan* by John Bevere. This book goes into great detail about the importance and value of forgiveness.

This exercise guides you through the process so that you can forgive and have a place in time to mark when your offense was released from your soul. Walk through this exercise with all those on your offender list. It might include your dad and mom, your spouse, and any others who have hurt you.

This exercise has three steps to it. So select one offender and go through the process. Do this exercise while you are home alone. You will need two kitchen chairs.

THE FORGIVENESS EXERCISE

1. Assume the role of the offender.

Place the two chairs facing each other. Pick a chair and sit facing the other chair. We'll call the chair in which you are sitting "chair A."

While you are sitting in chair A, role-play your offender. You are now this person. As you role-play this individual, have him or her apologize and ask for forgiveness for all that they have done to you. They are hypothetically confessing to you in the other chair (chair B). If I were doing this exercise about my dad, I would sit in chair A as I role-played my dad. I would verbally own his sin, apologize, and ask for forgiveness for the things I did and didn't do to Doug in chair B.

As I play my dad, I might say, "Doug, I need you to forgive me of..." Now since I am playing my dad, I can say what he needs to say to me in order to own and apologize for his sin against my life.

2. Role-play your response as the one offended.

Now I have played my dad as he asked forgiveness for several offenses against Doug, who was symbolically sitting in chair B. Yet as the one offended, I heard my dad own his sin and ask forgiveness for it. Now I can start step two.

I begin by physically moving to sit in chair B, now role-playing myself.

After hearing my dad ask for forgiveness, I now decide how I will respond. Above all be honest. If you are not ready to forgive your offender, tell him or her.

You could say, "I'm just not ready to do this yet, but I will try again in a few weeks."

Whatever you do when you play yourself, don't be a phony or do what you think you *should* do. Do what is real.

If you are able to forgive your offender, then tell him or her. In our example, Doug is now talking to Dad in the opposite chair.

I could say, "Dad, I forgive you."

I could really release him from his abuse and neglect of my soul and the impact his actions had on my life.

If you forgave your offender, move to step three. If at this time you are not able to forgive your offender, get out your calendar and set up a date in about three to four weeks when you will try this exercise again. Do this every month to measure your progress until you are able to forgive.

3. Role-play the offender's response to forgiveness.

In our example, Doug has forgiven Dad. Now I physically get up and sit down in chair A again and play the role of my dad. Now it is Dad's turn to respond to Doug's forgiveness.

Dad (role-played by Doug) might say, "Thanks, Doug." When Dad is finished talking to Doug, the exercise is over.

Let's review:

1. Start in chair A as the offender asking for forgiveness.
2. Now sit in chair B as yourself and honestly respond to your offender's request for forgiveness.
3. If you have forgiven him or her, go back to chair A and play the offender responding to the forgiveness.

Comments

This can be a very emotional exercise for those with extremely abusive backgrounds, so have a box of tissues nearby. In addition, make sure the phone, doorbell, or anything else will not interrupt you. It will be important for you to stay focused.

Do this exercise only after you have completed the cleansing the temple exercise. Many individuals attempt to forgive before they heal. Jesus cleansed the temple before He issued the words, "Father, forgive them" (Luke 23:34). Cleansing comes first, then forgiveness.

In all these exercises, each offender gets his or her time in the chair with you. You must role-play each one and receive an individual apology from each. Don't role-play more than one offender in a day.

Releasing your offenders will free you if you complete your cleansing the temple work first. I have personally experienced much freedom through these exercises given to me by God. I didn't read about these exercises somewhere and Christianize them. They are exercises the Lord gave me in the process of healing myself so that I can heal others also.

As you do these exercises and move through forgiveness, especially toward your spouse, you can once again feel free to give, trust, and build. That's what it is about—removing all the roadblocks to intimacy. As you do this, the door will swing open to an entirely new and refreshing way of life.

Let's pray together:

Lord, help me to process my woundedness and to apply these exercises to my life. Comfort me, Lord, and lead me to still waters where I can drink of the intimacy that You have for me. In Jesus's name, amen.

Day 13

THREE DAILY EXERCISES

Pray together? _____ Yes _____ No

What did you pray?

_____

_____

_____

Feelings exercise? _____ Yes _____ No

He shared   _____

                (feeling #1)

and   _____

                (feeling #2)

She shared   _____

                (feeling #1)

and   _____

                (feeling #2)

Praise/nurture together? _____ Yes _____ No

He shared _____

          (praise #1)

She shared _____

          (praise #1)

He shared _____

          (praise #2)

She shared _____

          (praise #2)

Day 14

CHIPPING AWAY
RELATIONAL PLAQUE

*Therefore confess your sins to each other and pray
for each other so that you may be healed.*
—James 5:16

Now you're probably asking yourself, *"What do plaque and relationships have to do with each other?"* Couples who don't own sin for what sin really is will develop relational plaque over time. It can take years.

Eventually a husband and wife will both become aware of the distance that has developed between them, distance caused by unconfessed sin. They are no longer as honest as they once were. Silently they keep score of things they never talk about. Entitlements or "you owe me" attitudes begin to grow as well as other dysfunctional or unhealthy behaviors because of unconfessed sin.

For plaque not to build up in a relationship we need to be honest about being wrong. This is true both for the husband who put down his wife and for the wife who did not clearly communicate her lack of sexual interest.

Saying "I'm sorry" isn't quite the same as saying "I sinned against you by putting you down." When you lightly say, "I'm sorry," the other spouse may be thinking, "I'll bet you're sorry!" Never attempt to minimize your offense by apologizing lightly when you're wrong. Own all of what you have done and any consequences you know that have occurred because of this offense.

When asking for the forgiveness of sin becomes a part of a couple's regular interaction, they are on their way to a plaque-free relationship. You may need to literally practice asking each other for forgiveness so that it becomes a regular habit. Here's an exercise to help you do just that.

AN OWNING EXERCISE

A helpful exercise for dealing with historical plaque is called "an owning." Let's walk through it step-by-step. It is very important that you follow the directions carefully. If you decide to do an owning, make sure that you both agree to follow the guidelines specifically.

1. Make a list of the sins you "own."

We humans have a tendency to sin, and being married, we have a tendency to sin against each other. The only way to deal with sin is to own it, confess it, and be forgiven of it by God and by our spouse. In this step we will deal with simply the "owning it" part of our sin.

Husbands and wives, *separately* review your relationship history, including your relationship before marriage. Individually make a list of the sins *you* committed toward your spouse. Some of these sins are actions, others are attitudes, and some are promises that you haven't fulfilled. This is *your* list to make. *Do not* ask for your spouse's help in developing your list of sins.

If you are struggling with what to write, pray. Ask God to reveal your sins to you. You will find that long-forgotten actions and attitudes will come into your mind. When this occurs, God is helping you so that you might find healing. Be as painstakingly honest with yourself as possible in making your list.

2. Read your "owning" list to your spouse.

At an agreed-upon time when you and your spouse can be alone, sit in chairs facing each other. You may feel the need for support from a counselor, pastor, or very safe layperson. This is permitted.

If you plan to do this at home and have children, make sure they are not at home during step two. In addition, take the phone off of the hook or turn on the answering machine. This can be a very emotional exercise, so keep a box of tissues nearby.

When you are seated facing each other, have your personal list of sins available. The first person reads off one of his sins to the spouse. For clarity, let's suppose the husband starts; we will call him Harry.

Harry states, "I need you to forgive me for _____."

The wife has only two options at this point. She may respond in one of the following ways:

1. "I forgive you for that."
2. "I need some time on that one."

Again, these are *her only two responses.* During the exercise, if anyone begins to give feedback or ask questions, *please stop the exercise.* Let me give you two examples of how to do it correctly:

> Harry: "I need you to forgive me for embarrassing you in front of your sisters at Christmas last year."
>
> Alice: "I forgive you for that."
>
> Harry: "I need you to forgive me for embarrassing you in front of your sisters at Christmas last year."
>
> Alice: "I need more time on that one."

These are the only two options Alice can have to respond to Harry's request for forgiveness. Anything else is unacceptable. If you have a pastor or counselor involved, that individual should stop the person who wants to respond any differently. Alice is not required to forgive Harry of every sin during the exercise, but they both must stick to the two-response format.

During this exercise, you are both going to feel very vulnerable. If one spouse uses this time to injure the other, it means that the couple is not ready to do this exercise without someone else present. If this happens to you, agree on who needs to be present and schedule a later time to resume.

Here is an example of what you *should not do.*

> Harry: "I need you to forgive me for embarrassing you in
> front of your sisters."
>
> Alice: "I am not ever forgiving you for that," "I still hate
> you for that," "I forgive you, but you were a real
> jerk," or "Why did you do that anyway?"

I hope you get the point. If you are going to do this owning exercise, it must be done correctly. In our example, Harry stated his sins, then Alice responded. Next it is Alice's turn to ask for forgiveness. Here is what it looks like so far with Harry's response.

> Harry: "I need you to forgive me for [sin #1]."
>
> Alice: "I forgive you."
>
> Alice: "I need you to forgive me for [sin #1]."
>
> Harry: "I forgive you."
>
> Harry: "I need you to forgive me for [sin #2]."
>
> Alice: "I need more time on that one."
>
> Alice: "I need you to forgive me for [sin #2]."
>
> Harry: "I need more time on that one."

I think you get the idea that you rotate back and forth. Inevitably, one spouse's list will be longer for whatever reason, and this is normal. Then just allow the person with the longer list to continue to ask for forgiveness with the other spouse continuing to respond appropriately.

Note: While going through and responding to your spouse's sins, be honest. If you are not able to forgive something at this point in time, be honest and just say the appropriate response, "I need more time on that one." It is better to be honest in this exercise than to lie to yourself or your spouse regarding where you are on an issue. Lying to each other never deepens intimacy.

3. Wait at least seventy-two hours before discussing your responses.

When each person is finished with his list, take some time apart for a little while; an hour or so is appropriate. *Do not talk about the exercise!* Give yourself at least seventy-two hours before you talk about the things mentioned in this exercise. You both will be too emotionally raw to discuss this exercise immediately.

The goal for an owning is not to be forgiven but to own our side of the street. In most cases, about 90 percent of our sins are forgiven. The percentage that is not forgiven by either spouse is that person's own issue; they need to work this through. It doesn't mean a spouse is less kind, less generous, or un-Christian because he or she needs more time to heal or process before forgiving.

Most couples find the owning exercise a great way to clean up the old layers of built-up plaque. Countless couples I have worked with believe this exercise alone gave them hope for achieving the intimate relationship they desired.

Sin that is not owned or that goes unconfessed is a plaque builder. To stay plaque-free you must remain consciously aware of when you sin toward your spouse. Immediately ask for forgiveness so that plaque does not build back up in your precious relationship.

I know I will sin. I expect that I will continue to sin. Although I hope it grows less, I still need to humble myself and ask forgiveness of my spouse, my children, and others. As you do, continue this exercise in your relationships to stay free from the plaque of sin.

Plaque is a terrible thing to have in a relationship. Nevertheless, the blood of Christ has the power to forgive sin. As you forgive and are forgiven, God's grace can enter into your marriage for the rest of your days.

Day 14

THREE DAILY EXERCISES

Pray together? _____ Yes _____ No

What did you pray?

_____

_____

_____

Feelings exercise? _____ Yes _____ No

He shared _____

(feeling #1)

and _____

(feeling #2)

She shared _____

(feeling #1)

and _____

(feeling #2)

Praise/nurture together? _____ Yes _____ No

He shared   _____

                (praise #1)

She shared   _____

                (praise #1)

He shared   _____

                (praise #2)

She shared   _____

                (praise #2)

Week 2

PROGRESS NOTES

Record your progress for the week on your spiritual exercise of prayer.

Husband:	1	2	3	4	5	6	7
Wife:	1	2	3	4	5	6	7

Record your progress on your feelings exercise.

Husband:	1	2	3	4	5	6	7
Wife:	1	2	3	4	5	6	7

Record your progress on the praise and nurturing exercise.

Husband:	1	2	3	4	5	6	7
Wife:	1	2	3	4	5	6	7

Additional constructive thoughts, comments, and observations

_____

_____

_____

_____

WEEK 3

SEXUAL MAKEOVER

Day 15

UNDERSTANDING THE STAGES OF SEXUAL DEVELOPMENT

When I was a child, I talked like a child, I thought like a child, I reasoned like a child. When I became a man, I put childish ways behind me.
—1 CORINTHIANS 13:11

ALL OF US continue to develop sexually throughout our entire lives. Some of us experience healthy, informed growth. Unfortunately for others, their sexuality has suffered because of being misinformed about sex as they developed.

Let's look at three basic developmental stages of sexuality. Depending on the individual's emotional or behavioral development, an adult can sexually be in any one of these three stages. When we discuss a "sexual child" or "sexual adolescent," we are referring to an adult who exhibits behaviors or attitudes from this stage. This is very important, for not everyone who is an adult physically is automatically an adult spiritually, emotionally, financially, or sexually.

STAGE ONE—SEXUAL CHILDHOOD

An adult whose behavior and emotions are consistent with that of a child's, regardless of his or her age, will have beliefs about sex that are

115

childlike. An adult who behaves as a child doesn't really understand that he or she is a sexual being.

Such individuals tend to avoid sexual responsibility in their marriages. They rely on their spouse to initiate all sex and often put it off as much as possible. Adults who behave as children feel nonsexual. They are uncomfortable, awkward, and even ashamed when discussing sex. The notion that others might think that they are having sex would be very disconcerting, even if they have children. They neither want to read about it nor learn about it. They refuse to grow, experiment, or explore sexually.

The husband or wife in stage one whose behavior exhibits that of a sexual child gets very emotional and unreasonable when sex is discussed, even in a therapy session. Adults at age twenty, thirty, forty, or older can be stuck at stage one as a sexual child. If this individual doesn't want to talk about sexuality, he or she won't, and that's that!

Adults behaving as sexual children make it difficult for their spouses to reach higher levels of sexual intimacy. If you find yourself in these descriptions, try to reach beyond your fears and awkwardness so that you and your spouse can enjoy sexual adulthood together.

STAGE TWO—SEXUAL ADOLESCENCE

Those at stage two, the adolescent stage of sexual development, are all too willing to be sexual. They enjoy sex, but sex is primarily about them having a good time. Sexual adolescents are much more focused on their own pleasure.

This individual refers to the sex act as "it," "some," and other object-type terms. When sexual needs are not met when this person feels they ought to be, he or she may pout or get angry.

The husband or wife at the sexual adolescence stage rarely considers the thoughts, feelings, or sexual needs of the other spouse. In addition, the sexual adolescent is not beyond using emotional or physical bullying to manipulate the partner into having sex.

Those stuck at stage two are often disconnected emotionally and spiritually during the sex act. They are capable of one-dimensional sex only and believe that more is better.

Sexual adolescents can damage their spouse and actually train them not to enjoy sex. The husband or wife who is behaving as a sexual adolescent can grow beyond this stage, but it usually takes work to promote his or her heart and beliefs to sexual adulthood.

STAGE THREE—SEXUAL ADULTHOOD

Mature sexual adults accept their sexuality. They understand that sex is a normal ongoing and committed part of an adult marriage. They accept their fair share of sexual initiation in the marriage. Sexual adults give themselves spirit, soul, and body and receive their partner's sexuality as well.

A sexual adult couple recognizes that they will enjoy sex thousands of times throughout a lifetime together. Mature sexual adults learn to communicate their sexual needs, desires, and preferences, and they can be creative during sexual encounters within the limits of their personalities. Feelings about sexuality can be discussed without shaming, blaming, or belittling the other spouse.

Manipulation is unnecessary to get sexual needs met. Sexual adults can keep their word and follow through with their sexual promises and agreements.

Sexuality can be a real blessing when both husband and wife are in stage three as sexual adults. They can talk about sex, negotiate with each other about sex, and hear each other during a sexual dialogue.

Of course, reaching sexual adulthood—as with spiritual, emotional, or financial adulthood—takes time, correct information, and a willingness to grow. As we read earlier, all things are possible in Christ Jesus. He can carry us from stage one through stage three into sexual adulthood. His grace, love and patience are with us as we ask Him to change us, and they are available to all who ask.

God can help you to attain sexual adulthood. Even if your sexual journey has been challenging, your soul will rest when both you and your spouse are at stage three of sexual adulthood.

Don't use this information about the stages of sexuality as ammunition to aim at your spouse. Instead, use it for your own self-awareness. If areas of your spouse's sexual struggle have been revealed, use this information as points of prayer, not points of manipulation.

In my own life, I laid down my sexuality before the Lord Jesus Christ and made Him Lord of it. It was at that point that I realized I was really free. When I have issues about sex, I don't talk to my wife first. I talk to my God. He is able to change me or change her or change us both. This is the quickest way to remove sexual blocks and hindrances between couples.

Both you and your spouse need to yield your sexuality to God as you mature sexually. You are probably going to have sex for the rest of your life. Sexual intimacy is a journey, not a destination. As you walk out that journey together, learning to balance your sexual personalities, personal preferences, and sexual maturity, you will soon discover that you never arrive. Sexual intimacy is a constantly evolving, wonderful journey of exploring and celebrating each other all the days of your life.

Please pray with me.

Jesus, I want what You want for my spouse and me sexually. I want to be as sexually mature as You can make me. Please intervene in my life and marriage, and open my eyes of understanding to sexually love, accept, and nurture my spouse. Amen.

Day 15

THREE DAILY EXERCISES

Pray together? _____ Yes _____ No

What did you pray?

_____

_____

_____

Feelings exercise? _____ Yes _____ No

He shared _____

         (feeling #1)

   and _____

         (feeling #2)

She shared _____

         (feeling #1)

   and _____

         (feeling #2)

Praise/nurture together? _____ Yes _____ No

He shared   _____

        (praise #1)

She shared   _____

        (praise #1)

He shared   _____

        (praise #2)

She shared   _____

        (praise #2)

Day 16

THE IMPACT OF
SEXUAL HISTORIES

The body is not meant for sexual immorality, but for the Lord, and the Lord for the body.... Do you not know that he who unites himself with a prostitute is one with her in body? For it is said, "The two will become one flesh."... Flee from sexual immorality. All other sins a man commits are outside his body, but he who sins sexually sins against his own body.

—1 CORINTHIANS 6:13–18

SEXUALITY IS AT the core of all of us. Sex should be a beautiful exchange between loving spouses. Unfortunately, some of us never developed a healthy and strong sense of sexuality because of past histories marked with issues such as sexual abuse or sexual addiction. Some marriages are also plagued with sexual anorexia, which is the active withholding of spiritual, emotional, and sexual intimacy. Such sexual baggage can create roadblocks to sexual and nonsexual intimacy in a marriage.

Most people probably have had some sexual history prior to marriage. If you abstained from sex prior to marriage, this is ideal. I praise God that you kept yourself just for your mate. However, I have met few couples for whom this was true of both spouses.

Your sexual history is exactly that—yours. Still, your premarital sexual behaviors may now be creating hindrances to your sexuality in your present relationship. Some premarital sexual behaviors may have been choices you made, while others may not have been choices at all but the result of sexual abuse. First, I will discuss the sexual experiences that were your choices. Sexual abuse and other experiences over which you had no control will be discussed later.

Before you were married, you may have had sex. If you are a Christian, you may have experienced a good degree of guilt over such sexual encounters. You may have become a committed Christian later on in life after many sexual experiences. Or you may have been a Christian who was educated by prevailing sexual attitudes and not fully awakened to Christian beliefs regarding the whole issue. Now, as you mature as a Christian, you view your earlier sexual choices as sin that was destructive to the lives of those you touched.

If you have a sexual history, evaluate what your experiences taught you about sex and measure that against what God's Word teaches. You can and must heal from the robbery of that sin, which attempts to keep you from the best sex of your life with your spouse.

Because of the painful nature of some of our sexual pasts, we may have a tendency to perpetuate the damage even once we've become mature Christians. Such painful baggage brought into a marriage is damaging on several levels.

Keeping a secret place

You feel that if you were totally honest, you would be rejected. Therefore you keep a secret place that you believe your spouse can't know about, can't love, and can't accept about you. This secret place damages the spiritual, emotional, and sexual intimacy within the relationship because you are not 100 percent available for intimacy. A certain percentage of yourself remains hidden.

Learned manipulation

The approaches you learned to get sex or avoid it are usually the only methods you know to bring into the relationship. Manipulation, such as lying and insensitive attitudes toward your spouse's sexuality, creep into the marriage.

Comparing previous partners

The sexual expectations to which you may have become accustomed can now be totally inappropriate for the sexual personality of your spouse. You may have experienced multiple sexual partners, along with their unique sexual personalities. You can project the memory of another's sexual personality onto your spouse. Outwardly you may not say anything, but inwardly you may question why your spouse can't sexually be more like someone else.

Projecting past sexual personalities onto your present spouse is the result of sin. It was sin for you to be involved with your past sexual partners, regardless of whether or not you knew better at the time. Sin exposed you to various sexual personalities and sexual fantasies. This sin can block you from accepting and appreciating the great sexual personality of your spouse.

Let's take a moment to talk about wants and needs in your relationship. I love a God who knows what you need better than you do yourself. In your distorted, sin-filled youth, you may have wanted a woman sexually to be a risk-taker and adventurous. Such sexual personalities tend to come with a lot of baggage that you probably wouldn't want in your life. What you may need is a woman who hasn't been sexual with anyone else, who loves you, and for whom you will never have to spend one minute wondering if she has been unfaithful.

I am so grateful that God knows what we need. Many of us are too ignorant to know what is best for us. I have talked with many men and women who defile their marriages with the sexual expectations created by sin. They loudly complain about what they want from their spouses because of their earlier exposure to sexual sin.

Your sexual memories, whether you like it or not, are the unfortunate consequence of the sins to which you exposed yourself. Your memory is your problem. Don't project it onto your spouse.

Often couples defile their present marriage with a past sinful experience or expectation. If your spouse is pressuring you because of a sinful past by comparing you to it, ask him or her to talk to God to deal with that expectation.

One of the reasons you married your spouse is because you liked his or her personality. Now you need to practice being grateful for your spouse and for his or her sexual expression. Your partner may not have the same past as you do. As you journey together, you can create your own special sexual history together.

YOUR OWN SEXUAL HISTORY AS A COUPLE

As a married couple, not only do you have sexual histories with others prior to marriage, but you have also created your own sexual history within your present marriage. For some, this history is mostly positive despite a few minor bumps that need to be worked out. For others who may have been married for decades, there may seem to be more bumps through the years than anything else.

Some husbands and wives had to learn, as all of us do, through trial and error, but communication was good, and you managed to pull through. Other couples have experienced major setbacks within their relationships that have created spiritual and emotional roadblocks to sexual intimacy.

Some couples have experienced marital sexual abuse or what is now called "mate rape." The wife clearly didn't want to have sex, but the husband forced himself on her. Other partners have been sexually rejected so often that they no longer even want sex. Some couples I have counseled have been involved in watching pornography together and even have had others who were sexually involved with them. Many couples have had affairs, prostitutes, or homosexual encounters during their marriage, which are all now a part of their marital sexual history.

The sexual histories of some couples are laden with more baggage within their marriages than before. Years of being sexually shamed, ridiculed, or put down can substantially limit spiritual, emotional, and sexual intimacy. Couples with these issues within their marriage will have more difficulty working through the blockages to intimacy than most. Nevertheless, it will be necessary to receive healing to improve your intimacy.

I don't believe in minimizing the role of your past sexual history. The past is valid, real, and important to be owned. As you take responsibility to heal from the past, your likelihood of spiritual, emotional, and physical intimacy in the future is improved.

Sometimes religious people say, "The past is the past. Forgive it and move on." Oftentimes the person saying it is the offender, not the recipient. If a person gets shot and a bullet remains in his body, you wouldn't tell him to forgive first, would you? No. First you would get him to a doctor to remove the bullet. Even if he cried out to the offender, "I forgive you," while in pain, he would still need to have the bullet taken out.

Once the "bullet" (your sexual past) is taken out, you can begin to heal and really release the past. Even if you have been wounded to the core of your sexual being by your spouse, given information and time, you can heal and begin to move on.

Day 16

THREE DAILY EXERCISES

Pray together? _____ Yes _____ No

What did you pray?

_____

_____

_____

Feelings exercise? _____ Yes _____ No

He shared   _____

               (feeling #1)

    and   _____

               (feeling #2)

She shared   _____

               (feeling #1)

    and   _____

               (feeling #2)

Praise/nurture together? _____ Yes _____ No

He shared _____

(praise #1)

She shared _____

(praise #1)

He shared _____

(praise #2)

She shared _____

(praise #2)

Day 17

OVERCOMING SEXUAL ABUSE AND SEXUAL ADDICTIONS

For everyone born of God overcomes the world. This is the victory that has overcome the world, even our faith. Who is it that overcomes the world? Only he who believes that Jesus is the Son of God.
—1 JOHN 5:4–5

SEXUAL ABUSE AFFECTS each victim differently. For some victims it brings on a lifestyle of *hypersexuality*, or a tendency to be sexual all the time. The effect of sexual abuse on another might be *hyposexuality*, where the individual is not sexual at all. Some men and women who have been sexually abused struggle with depression, eating disorders, rage, and the inability to enjoy healthy relationships. Many suffer with addictions throughout their lives.

Many books and journal articles have been written on the effects of sexual abuse. For some individuals it appears that the abuse has not affected them much at all. They appear to be more resilient to the adverse affects. Some are affected by the abuse for a period of time but seem to work through the issues. Still others who have been sexually abused desperately need healing in their soul to process the pain and the memories. This person may need professional help to work through these past events. All are valid responses to this trauma.

If you fall into this last category, your offender has already stolen many years of your life. I strongly encourage you to seek professional help to get the healing you need. I am a survivor of sexual abuse, and I believe that talking about it to someone else tremendously reduces the shame it causes. I made a decision to work through my misconception of sexuality and to deal with the rage it caused. My healing process allowed me to put the past in the past and not let it control my worth, value, or sexuality.

Just remember that you didn't cause or ask for sexual abuse to happen. You are in no way responsible for what happened. Nevertheless, you are 100 percent responsible for your healing. I know it's possible! I have seen many others throughout my years as a practicing counselor find healing from sexual abuse and its effect on their marital relationships.

As you heal—spirit, soul, and body—you will have more of yourself to give to your spouse and to your children. If this applies to you, outline what you feel you need to do, and pray and ask the Lord to free you from the past by directing you into the path of healing that you need.

THE HIDDEN SHAME OF SEXUAL ADDICTIONS

Sexual addiction is a killer of spiritual, emotional, and sexual intimacy for married couples. It mostly involves a habitual viewing of porno-graphic material along with masturbation. Even though most sex addicts are men, the numbers are increasing for women sex addicts.

Spouses of sex addicts are definitely affected by the addiction just as much as the sex addict themselves. They most likely suffer from depres-sion and low self-esteem. From my professional experience, I can assure you that as long as the addict is active in his addiction, he cannot be intimate. The addict is usually emotionally limited and crippled with guilt and shame. An addict can be a deacon, a pastor, or a Sunday school teacher, but he can't be intimate with his wife on an ongoing basis.

If this might be an issue for you, or if you are wondering whether or not you are married to a sex addict, get more information and begin the process of healing. This addiction is a plague in America. I strongly believe that it is becoming the number-one hindrance keeping couples from enjoying God's blessing of spiritual, emotional, and physical intimacy.

SEXUAL ANOREXIA

Sexual anorexia is the withholding of spiritual, emotional, and physical intimacy from a spouse. A sexually anorexic spouse will refuse to be available to share feelings, be sexual, to pray together, and will rarely be affectionate. Sexual anorexia is very covert. Often you may not even realize it has been going on for many years.

Sexual anorexia runs counter to the goal of three-dimensional intimacy. The following is an excerpt from my video *Sexual Anorexia*, which helps identify this pattern in your relationship. Answer these questions with your spouse as truthfully as possible.

SEXUAL ANOREXIC PATTERNS

❏ Yes ❏ No 1. Does it feel as if your spouse limits or withholds love from you?

❏ Yes ❏ No 2. Does it feel as if your spouse limits or withholds the amount of praise he or she gives you?

❏ Yes ❏ No 3. Does it feel as if your spouse limits or withholds the amount of sex he or she gives you?

❏ Yes ❏ No 4. Does it feel as if your spouse is unwilling or unable to share his or her feelings with you?

❏ Yes ❏ No 5. Does it feel as if your spouse uses anger or silence to control the relationship?

❏ Yes ❏ No 6. Does it feel as if your spouse has unfounded or ongoing criticism of you?

❏ Yes ❏ No 7. Does your spouse control or shame you about money issues?

❏ Yes ❏ No 8. Do you or your spouse tend to keep yourselves so busy that you have little time for just you as a couple (just couple time without other family members present)?

❏ Yes ❏ No 9. If issues or problems come up in the relationship, do you tend to get blamed before your spouse owns an issue?

If you or your spouse answered yes to five or more questions, I would recommend that you seek help in this area. Sexual anorexia is similar to an eating disorder. It is stubborn, but there is practical help available to get out and stay out of these harmful sexual anorexic patterns.

If your spouse is sexually anorexic, whether it is the husband or the wife, you probably feel very alone. You may feel like roommates instead of marriage partners. The spouse of an anorexic often feels avoided, confused, dry on the inside, and may feel more like the manager of the household, not the love of her or his life.

Many spouses of anorexics feel they are not valuable and have finally just given up on intimacy because deep down inside he or she knows that if it came down to being intimate or leaving the marriage, the anorexic would chose leaving.

I have counseled many women married to male anorexics, and their souls were now almost hollow from the lack of praise from their husbands. They haven't been praised in years, and some have not been sexual in months or years. They are often angry, confused, and have feelings of hopelessness.

The husband of a sexual anorexic wife often is hostile from trying to be perfect enough to be loved or to be sexually intimate. Jesus can and will walk a couple through this issue of sexual anorexia regardless of how dry they may presently feel. I have seen this miracle of healing occur in marriages with anorexia present.

There is hope for those who struggle with sexual addiction and sexual anorexia. If an individual will do the work of healing, miracles of intimacy can occur.

SEX ON THE NET

As people living in a culture obsessed with technology, we need to address the Internet in the context of marital intimacy. The Internet is a great tool for research, shopping, and many other services. Like the television, it can be used for good purposes, such as carrying the gospel around the world. It can also be used for less noble purposes.

The largest portion of the Internet is devoted to pornography. Pornography in all its forms, including magazines and videos, is a real threat to intimacy. Internet pornography is an even greater threat. Pornography on the Internet is more perverse than what you can purchase anywhere. It is available twenty-four hours a day, seven days a week, and it is also much more addictive than any other form of pornography.

In the past five years I have encountered increasing numbers of men and women who are getting into trouble through chat rooms, news groups, pornography, and sex services. The Internet is trapping people from all walks of life—including missionaries, pastors, Bible scholars, and Christian celebrities.

The Bible warns us to flee sexual temptation (1 Cor. 6:18). To own a computer with open access in a home with young people is unwise. If you need or want Internet access at your home, you must protect yourself. One option available on our website www.intimatematters.com is what I believe to be one of the best porn-blockers on the net. There are no passwords, and you cannot delete the filter unless you handwrite a letter to the company. With this in place, Internet porn cannot accidentally traumatize teenagers or adults. If you have Internet access, I strongly encourage you to download the filter today.

The Internet can be addictive not only for pornography but also for games. If your marriage's intimacy is being threatened by the Internet, you will need to address this issue together. Work together to establish boundaries to protect the precious gift of intimacy in your marriage.

In the space provided write out your boundaries for the Internet.

OUR INTERNET AGREEMENT

Our Internet agreement for our marriage is:

_____

_____

_____

_____

IN CONCLUSION

Sexual matters need to be addressed by both spouses. Our sexual histories, sexual personalities, sexual development, sexual addictions, and sexual anorexia can all be overcome by the grace of our God and a willingness to obey Him in our areas of need.

Day 17

THREE DAILY EXERCISES

Pray together? _____ Yes _____ No

What did you pray?

_____

_____

_____

Feelings exercise? _____ Yes _____ No

He shared _____

            (feeling #1)

and _____

            (feeling #2)

She shared _____

            (feeling #1)

and _____

            (feeling #2)

Praise/nurture together? _____ Yes _____ No

He shared   _____

        (praise #1)

She shared   _____

        (praise #1)

He shared   _____

        (praise #2)

She shared   _____

        (praise #2)

DAY 18

THE JOY OF SEXUAL ACCEPTANCE

Let your fountain be blessed, and rejoice with the wife of your youth. As a loving deer and a graceful doe, let her breasts satisfy you at all times; and always be enraptured with her love.

—PROVERBS 5:18–19, NKJV

A STRONG SEX DRIVE that doesn't quit until near death is a gift from God to men. A man's sexual drive forces him to push through his insecurities and self-doubts to start dating. It is also a large motivator for men to marry. This drive compels men to work through marital issues with their wives. This sexual gift from God is what glues a man to a woman spiritually, emotionally, and neurologically.

The gift of sex is different for women. The woman's drive seems to come mostly from the communion in an emotional and spiritual realm. Generally speaking, when she feels close, she wants to express herself physically. She is not looking for a sex act; she is looking for a love event during sexuality. I believe women intuitively desire spirit, soul, and body sex for the majority of their sexual experiences. This gift of sexuality and communion from her soul is as important to acknowledge as the husband's physiological sex drive.

It is important that you never attempt to manipulate or change how your husband or wife is created. If you can learn to accept your spouse sexually, you will move much more quickly toward creating the best sex of your life.

I vividly remember a conversation I was having with a man one day about his sexuality with his wife. He was a forty-seven-year-old blue-collar worker with six boys and a wife who worked at a garment factory. They were having sex very infrequently. He and I started talking about the emotional needs of women. He said to me, "You're right!" Apparently about a year ago he read a book about women and what they need. He said the book told him to listen without trying to solve the problem. It said to ask questions about her feelings and to also share things about his life without being prompted. He told me, "I did everything the book told me to do for three months. That's when we were having the most and best sex of our marriage!" I asked him what happened. He said something that has stuck with me all these years: "I stopped doing my part."

For three months this husband accepted the fact that men are different from women. Women have needs that men don't necessarily have at the same level. Some men are pretty simple in their thought processes about sex. A major part of a woman's sexuality is wrapped up in her getting her spiritual and emotional needs met on a daily basis. When this happens, a man will see the transformation of his wife's spiritual, emotional, and sexual demeanor. If you give your wife the oil of intimacy, you will find that sexuality is more comfortable for her to participate in and initiate.

No Magic Buttons

There are no magic buttons on your wife that can get you more sex. Some women have not matured into sexual adults and still behave as sexual children. It's possible to be a prince of a guy for a year and still have no increased sexual expression from your wife. In cases like this, definitely pursue professional help.

Moving on toward the husband's side of the relationship, some men are sexual, and most are very sexual. This will not change! They love to be touched and to touch. They love your beauty, your body, and sexuality together. They think about sex almost as much as they think about food. Men are generally creatures of appetite, and most women were aware of this long before marriage.

Imagine taking your husband to the mall early the day after Thanksgiving to go Christmas shopping. You know the sales are great, and you plan to accomplish a great deal because stores are open from 7:00 a.m. (or earlier!) to 10:00 p.m. Your husband is running a little behind, so he forgets to eat breakfast.

Ten o'clock approaches, and he starts hinting about lunch. You continue to shop as eleven o'clock approaches, and your husband indicates more firmly that he's getting hungry. Again, you pacify him and assure him that you will eat soon. Twelve o'clock now goes by, and this fairly nice man you married is getting rude—you can tell food is increasingly occupying his thoughts. By one o'clock he's a monster. He won't say anything, and he is mad! He is totally fixated on food, and if you don't stop and eat soon, not only is shopping over, but it's going to be a bad day for everyone.

Ladies, you know what I am talking about. We call it male "food anxiety." We wake up wanting to know what's for breakfast. At ten thirty in the morning we want to know what's for lunch. When we come home from work, you know what the classic male greeting is: "Hi, honey. What's for dinner?" You would think we have little else on or minds. If men don't know when they are eating, they get food anxiety. If you don't think this is true, try not telling your husband when and what he is eating and see what happens.

I think we clearly illustrated that most men who are not depressed or sexually anorexic are appetite-driven. This will not change, for it is the gift of God. An appetite for life in general makes men work harder, create more, and keep working, because if you don't work, you don't have money for food!

What does all this food talk have to do with sex? Food is a classic way to illustrate that, like food, men think a lot about sex. Most have heard the urban myths about how often men think about sex. Although

I have never personally read these studies, I think the point is, we think about sex a lot.

Now, if a man is in a manipulation-based sexual system, then he must rely on his fine-tuned skills to manipulate his wife into sex. Living like this keeps most men in a constant state of "sexual anxiety." They don't know when they are having sex or if they are ever having sex again. This kind of system produces more sexual anxiety, which causes men to think about it even more.

Ladies, what I am telling you is the truth. I have counseled men for many years on sexual issues. When men know when sex will occur and who will initiate it, they will think about sex much less and experience almost no sexual anxiety.

Once two sexual adults in a marriage arrive at a place of sexual agreement, peace floods into the sexual system. We are talking about accepting men sexually where they are. You won't change his desire for sex, and if you try to manipulate him in this area, it can create passive or aggressive conflict in the marriage. Remember that male sexuality is a gift from God. It is to be celebrated by the couple, not tolerated. A man who is sexually tolerated by his wife will, over time, generate many negative feelings toward his wife. A man who generally feels sexual acceptance and is sexually celebrated will have an ongoing positive feeling and expression of love for his wife.

On the other hand, a husband who ignores the spiritual and emotional aspects of his wife will also damage their sexuality over time. The man who is spiritually and emotionally lazy has a huge surprise down the road. The surprise is that she won't be interested, and it will be because you did not accept her sexually and emotionally.

If you want your wife to reject sex, don't pray with her, listen to her feelings, or keep your word outside the bedroom. They laugh, but those who have refused to sexually accept their wife's intimacy needs know I am telling the truth.

EMBRACING YOUR SEXUAL PERSONALITIES

Issues pertaining to sexual preferences, sexual appetites, and sexual differences often come up during marriage counseling sessions. At these times I like to bring up what I call "sexual personalities."

Our sexual personality is often very similar to our nonsexual personality. If you marry a woman who drives the speed limit, doesn't take many risks, and is pretty conservative in her beliefs and behaviors, don't expect her sexual personality to be exotic or bizarre. She probably won't be what you created in your imagination as a teenager. She will be herself.

Men, take a minute here and think about this. Is your wife more conservative in her approach to life, or is she more appetite driven? Is she a risk taker? Is she loud? Whatever her personality is outside the bedroom, it will most likely be her personality inside your bedroom, regardless of your preconceived notions of what she should be. She is who she is. Accepting her sexual personality will give you a better perspective of your precious spouse.

Ladies, if you married a man who likes to take risks, drives fast, lives on the edge, and is creative in his work and life, then these characteristics may also be a part of his sexual personality. If such traits do not reflect his personality outside the bedroom, then I doubt that he would be different in the bedroom.

Having laid that groundwork, now the fun begins! Often men or women who take risks and have more aggressive personalities are attracted to more stable spouses who do not seek the limelight. You can see how these personalities complement each other in most areas of life. When it comes to sex, both the husband and wife will desire sexual expression that is congruent with their personalities.

Your partner's personality is a gift that can balance your sexual intimacy as a couple. Accepting each other as a gift is important in this process of negotiating what your sexual expression can be. Both personalities are challenged to grow and yet stay true to themselves. Genuine balance can take years to negotiate. This is especially true when a couple polarizes, which occurs when each demands to be right instead of both personalities growing sexually into oneness.

We will get more specific about solutions and negotiations with sexuality later in the guide. For now I simply want to make you aware of sexual personalities and how they rarely differ from our nonsexual personalities.

Day 18

THREE DAILY EXERCISES

Pray together? _____ Yes _____ No

What did you pray?

_____

_____

_____

Feelings exercise? _____ Yes _____ No

He shared   _____
                 (feeling #1)

        and   _____
                 (feeling #2)

She shared   _____
                 (feeling #1)

        and   _____
                 (feeling #2)

Praise/nurture together? _____ Yes _____ No

He shared   _____

        (praise #1)

She shared   _____

        (praise #1)

He shared   _____

        (praise #2)

She shared   _____

        (praise #2)

Day 19

CREATING SEXUAL AGREEMENT

*Let the husband render to his wife the affection due her, and like-
wise also the wife to her husband. The wife does not have authority
over her own body, but the husband does. And likewise the husband
does not have authority over his own body, but the wife does.
Do not deprive one another except with consent for a time.*

—1 CORINTHIANS 7:3–5, NKJV

A SEXUAL AGREEMENT OCCURS when a couple intelligently and calmly discusses how often they both desire to have sexual intimacy and then fairly distributes the responsibility for initiating sex. The husband and wife decide verbally and then record how they want to structure their sexuality so that both are reasonably happy.

Reasonably is a very important word. Life is about negotiation. This is especially true in a marriage. If a man is pestering his wife to have sex daily, or if the wife only wants sex once a month, they are both being sexually selfish and unreasonable.

In sexual agreement, we must apply the Amos 3:3 principle that says that two must agree to walk together. If you don't agree on a sexual system, you will still create one without really agreeing about it. Although unusual, some couples create a naturally evolved sexual system between them that works quite well.

144

CREATING A SEXUAL AGREEMENT

Sexual systems are an issue that many couples fight over for decades. As you walk through the process of creating a sexual agreement together, I will ask you to do three things.

1. Be open-minded to each other's sexual needs.
2. Be honest about your sexuality.
3. If you can't do this together, get professional help.

The first step toward creating a sexual agreement is the issue of frequency. First, both of you will need to write on a piece of paper your own personal preferences for frequency. The average couple enjoys sexual relations one, two, three, or more times a week for couples up to the age of about fifty. After fifty, sexual intimacy usually decreases to about once a week. I'm providing this information as a reference point because I am asked this question so often.

Now you must share what you've written and begin negotiating. This is *your* marital sexual system, so you can be as creative as you desire. How can you handle differing desires? Here's one way: if he prefers two sexual experiences each week and she wants to be sexual three times a week, then on his week he can have his desired frequency and on her week she can choose hers.

Before you go any further, check off the box below saying that you have thus far agreed on the frequency of sex.

☐ We have agreed on sexual frequency.

Remember that this is *your* sexual agreement. I usually ask couples to stick to their agreements for a minimum of ninety days to see if the system works for both partners. If the system needs changing at that point, discuss it at a restaurant or in another public place. Don't discuss it in your bedroom or any other place in your house so that one spouse doesn't attempt to pressure the other into more or less sexual intimacy than they agreed to.

The following are several basic sexual systems for you to choose from. You may come up with your own version of a system, which is fine. As a couple has children, raises those children, and then goes through the stage of the children leaving the home, the sexual systems will change. Nevertheless, both must continue to agree on the changes.

System one

After you have agreed on your sexual frequency, you will now simply need to select the days that you want to be sexual. If you want to be sexual twice a week, then you can pick any two days of the week that work for your schedule; for example, Tuesday and Saturday or Wednesday and Sunday.

In this system you can divide the responsibility to initiate sex by the day or by the week.

Here's an example of dividing by the day: Let's suppose Jason and Dana choose to be sexual two days a week on Tuesday and Saturday. Jason could be responsible to initiate on Tuesdays, and Dana could be responsible for initiating on Saturdays.

Here's an example of dividing responsibility by the week: on the first and third week of the month, Jason would initiate; on the second and fourth week, Dana would initiate the sexual encounters.

Many busy couples love this system because once it is in place, they don't have to think about it. It easily fits into a busy schedule because they are both stress free concerning sexuality. Other couples find this system too rigid and lacking in spontaneity.

System two

System two is a little less rigid. In this system you would split the week up between the two of you. If you agreed on having sex twice a week, then Jason could choose either Sunday, Monday or Tuesday for the day in which he wants to initiate sex. However, he would have to initiate sex one time during this three-day period.

Wednesday would be a day off for both of you in a two-times-a-week system. Some couples make Wednesday a day that either can ask. If you chose to have sex two to three times a week, or simply three times a week, then try keeping Wednesday as a day that either can ask.

Dana would initiate sex once during the three-day period of Thursday, Friday, and Saturday. So Jason has his part of the week to initiate, and Dana has her part of the week. They are both clear regarding what days to initiate and who is responsible to initiate.

This system allows flexibility for a person to choose when they want to be sexual. Again, some couples love this system, but for others this system would not work.

System three

System three is a rotating system. In this system if you decide to have sex twice a week, each person will have up to three days to initiate sex with the other spouse. You can initiate within any of your days.

Following the third day of the week, it becomes the other spouse's turn. This spouse now has up to three days to initiate sex.

In this system, Jason has three days to initiate. If he decides to wait until day two, then fine. Following day two, after they have sex it immediately becomes Dana's turn.

Now it's Dana's turn. She can initiate sex on the very first day of her three-day period, or she can wait until day three.

Dana decides to initiate the very next day. Now Dana's turn is over, and the next day it is Jason's turn. He just had sex two days in a row, so he may wait to initiate.

This system provides both partners the most flexibility and is especially successful for those couples seeking spontaneity. It also accommodates couples who are seeking a greater frequency of sexuality in their relationship.

In this system, you can have sex as little as twice a week (when both partners wait for the third day to initiate), daily, or anywhere in between. This system is ideal for some couples, but for others it is too fluid.

These are the three basic sexual agreement systems. Your coupleship is unique, so you can choose any of these three systems or come up with a sexual system of your own. The sexual system you choose—one, two, three, or your own—isn't as important as the fact that you walk in agreement sexually.

Sexual agreement is a blessing. You will be married a long, long time, and it is better to agree about sex, negotiate, and change systems over time than to have an unknown sexual system that neither one of you wants. Implementing this chapter can give you genuine sexual harmony and peace.

As a Christian marriage and family counselor, I know that where the Spirit of the Lord is, there can be peace. Too often Christian marriages do not reflect this peace in the bedroom. But it's not because of a lack of love or even a lack of sexual desire—it is often because of a lack of agreement.

THE BENEFITS OF AGREEMENT

- Clarity and peace in marriage

- Reduced sexual anxiety, fear of rejection, and inclination to manipulate spouse

- Husband won't feel that he is expected to be the primary sexual initiator

- Wife won't feel that her own sexuality is submerged beneath her husband's and will have a new sense of autonomy

- Wife will be freer to relax not only sexually but also with physical affection such as her husband's spontaneous hugs and kisses

- Couple as a unit will find that their intimacy will significantly increase

148

- Couple will experience a heightened sense of sexual esteem and sexual confidence

- No one person will have complete sexual authority

During these thirty days, I trust your own experience will be positive as you and your spouse learn to walk together in sexual agreement. Even though a sexual agreement may be challenging for some who have been living irresponsibly as sexual children or sexual adolescents, the journey to maturity is well worth it.

Day 19

THREE DAILY EXERCISES

Pray together? _____ Yes _____ No

What did you pray?

_____

_____

_____

Feelings exercise? _____ Yes _____ No

He shared _____

(feeling #1)

    and _____

(feeling #2)

She shared _____

(feeling #1)

    and _____

(feeling #2)

Praise/nurture together? _____ Yes _____ No

He shared _____

(praise #1)

She shared _____

(praise #1)

He shared _____

(praise #2)

She shared _____

(praise #2)

Sexuality: Spouse's turn today is

husband's _____ wife's _____

Day 20

GUIDELINES FOR A SUCCESSFUL SEXUAL AGREEMENT

Marriage should be honored by all, and the marriage bed kept pure,
for God will judge the adulterer and all the sexually immoral.
—HEBREWS 13:4

BELOW ARE SOME guidelines for a successful sexual agreement. You can use these guidelines to answer any questions you may have.

1. Always say yes.

My advice: *Always say yes* unless you have a doctor's excuse! This may seem extreme until you understand this agreement.

When it's the other person's turn, comply with his or her advances. When it's your turn, your partner should comply with yours as well. We all know when our spouse is truly too sick to be sexual, and we must be considerate of that. But I want to be clear; there are *no excuses*! "I'm tired" or "I have a headache" does not work in this arrangement.

Do not manipulate or withhold sex from each other. These behaviors are enemies of intimacy that will destroy the momentum and closeness of the relationship during these thirty days.

Realize that not everyone who says he or she wants intimacy really does. There is no greater way to create chaos and anger than for a spouse to break his or her word regarding sex.

2. Impose consequences.

What do you do when your spouse doesn't keep his or her word after you've set up a sexual agreement? Before you begin or after your spouse fails two times to either initiate sexually or respond appropriately to your sexual advances, consequences *must be implemented* for change. Setting up consequences generally works better *before* you start a sexual system.

To work, consequences must be something negative a person would prefer not to do rather than have sex. Let me provide some examples that have been effective for other couples. Each spouse must choose his or her own consequence.

- Hand wash and detail the spouse's automobile
- Volunteer for two to four hours at a nursing home
- Send $100 to the local political party to which you are most opposed
- Volunteer at the local political party to which you are most opposed
- Spend time with a relative you dislike
- Send money to a relative or organization you don't like
- Run two miles
- Give your spouse a sixty- to ninety-minute massage
- Watch the children for four hours while your spouse goes somewhere
- Give up watching sports for two weeks
- Give up going hunting or fishing
- Make a counseling appointment

Each person must decide what their own consequence would be for not fully participating in the sexual agreement. If a person refuses to do their consequence, or if one person is regularly not keeping their word sexually, then I would strongly suggest a counseling session.

3. Respect each other's sexual space.

When it's *not* your turn, *you may not ask!* This is a simple guideline, but when someone consistently does not respect the sexual space of the other person, the sexual system can erode.

4. Determine how you will handle monthly cycles.

It is important for a couple to make a clear communication about what is expected or accepted during this time of the month. The couple also needs to communicate about when the wife needs to tell the spouse the news about the starting of the cycle.

Couples vary so much about sex and the cycle. For some couples, they just keep having intercourse, and for others, they wouldn't even consider sexual relations during this time. Options for couples seem to be one of the following:

1. Continue sexually as normal

2. Suspend sexual activity for a defined period (i.e., so many days or so many turns at initiating)

3. Be sexual but no intercourse

Any option is fine, but it is imperative that you both agree with the choice so that no misunderstandings occur.

Discuss and agree about how to communicate when a cycle begins. A couple decides when she is to communicate the change in their normal sexual expression. Some couples have designed an agreement system for communicating this information:

- As soon as she finds out, she will let her husband know.
- She sends an e-mail with a catchphrase.
- She mentions it when he comes home before dinner.
- She mentions it after dinner but before homework.

Clear communication can save both spouses ill feelings due to a change in routine. Usually ill feelings are the result of the *change* in the sexual agreement. So for the sake of both of you, take a preventative measure as you go through these thirty days.

5. Agree on sexual behaviors.

As we stated earlier, people vary in their sexual personalities, preferences, histories, and the amount of sexual behaviors they have participated in.

Since your sexuality is going to be the only garden of intimacy that you will both be eating from, it is helpful for you both to define what is acceptable. Some fruit, or types of expression, may be acceptable all the time, others may be acceptable on occasion, and some fruit is definitely forbidden. You also must determine who will initiate the sexual expression that is occasionally acceptable.

Again, this is your sexual garden. We are not addressing what is right or wrong but rather what *both* of you want in your garden. On a separate sheet of paper, write out the various fruits of your sexual expression that each of you desires. Below you can indicate what is acceptable for each spouse or both.

ACCEPTABLE SEXUAL BEHAVIOR

Example (fill in)	He (circle one)	She (circle one)
Position 1:	Yes No Only if I initiate	Yes No Only if I initiate
Position 2:	Yes No Only if I initiate	Yes No Only if I initiate
Act A:	Yes No Only if I initiate	Yes No Only if I initiate

Example (fill in)	He (circle one)	She (circle one)
Act B:	Yes No Only if I initiate	Yes No Only if I initiate
Place 1:	Yes No Only if I initiate	Yes No Only if I initiate
Place 2:	Yes No Only if I initiate	Yes No Only if I initiate

After you write all this out, both of you circle the appropriate response: "yes," "no," or "only if I initiate." Everything you both circle "yes" is a fruit that you both agree on and can participate in with a clear conscious before God and each other.

The things you both circle "no" are forms of expression that would be defiling to your particular garden and would not even be requested by either spouse.

The forms of sexual expression for which one circled "yes" and the other "no" are areas of sexual disagreement. These are forms of sexual expression you would not participate in or request during sex because you *both* do not agree.

If you feel these areas need further discussion, you can seek out a counselor or see a pastor in your area. The purpose of counseling would be to hear the rationales and histories to determine if such a sexual behavior is negotiable. The goal of counseling is never to manipulate your spouse into doing what you want sexually.

The option that states "only if I initiate" can be used by a spouse who realizes a mate enjoys a particular form of sexual expression. Still, this spouse does not want to feel obliged to always participate in this expression, except on occasion for the sake of the spouse.

Agreement on what fruits are acceptable to both partners can add a greater sense of safety and trust in the area of sexuality. Agreement results in sexual freedom and fun.

6. Both must agree before changing the system.

The system stays in place for at least sixty to ninety days before changing any aspect of it. One person cannot make changes in the sexual agreement. Both spouses must agree for a change to be made. If you feel you need a professional to navigate you through changes, please see one. Some couples agree to make changes in their sexual agreement only if their pastor or counselor also agrees. This minimizes any manipulation.

You now have outlined how to create a sexual system. On a separate sheet of paper, both of you need to write down your sexual system. Below is a checklist for you to include the various ingredients of a successful sexual agreement.

OUR SEXUAL AGREEMENT

☐ Our sexual agreement is written down in a clear format that outlines how often sex will occur.
☐ Our sexual agreement is written down and is clear regarding who is responsible for initiating sex.
☐ Our agreement states that we will say yes unless we have a doctor's excuse.
☐ Our sexual agreement includes self-imposed consequences for both spouses if either does not keep the agreement.
☐ We have included the not-asking-when-it's-not-your-turn policy.
☐ We have an agreed-upon plan regarding menstrual cycles and the communication of their onset.
☐ We have a written agreement regarding what is "acceptable," "not acceptable," and "only-if-I-initiate" behavior.
☐ We have a clause as to when our agreement can be changed.

If you completed all eight steps, you only have one more step to go. When do you want to get started? You can write the date in the space below or put it on your agreement.

Date started: _____

Living in Colorado, I've learned that hiking is work. But it seems the higher you climb, the cleaner the air, the cooler the temperature, and the more spectacular the view. I am very proud of you for taking the climb. I believe your intimacy will rise to a new level. I pray God's richest blessing on your marriage as you enjoy all the fruits you have agreed upon.

Day 20

THREE DAILY EXERCISES

Pray together? _____ Yes _____ No

What did you pray?

_____

_____

_____

Feelings exercise? _____ Yes _____ No

He shared   _____
              (feeling #1)

    and   _____
              (feeling #2)

She shared   _____
              (feeling #1)

    and   _____
              (feeling #2)

Praise/nurture together? _____ Yes _____ No

He shared   _____

               (praise #1)

She shared   _____

               (praise #1)

He shared   _____

               (praise #2)

She shared   _____

               (praise #2)

Sexuality: Spouse's turn today is

              husband's _____ wife's _____

Day 21

3-D SEX

Let him kiss me with the kisses of his mouth—for your love is more
delightful than wine. Pleasing is the fragrance of your perfumes; your
name is like perfume poured out.... Take me away with you.

—SONG OF SOLOMON 1:2–4

GOD CREATED SEX for procreation, but He also designed it for our enjoyment. Sexuality is a core part of each person's God-given role here on this earth. God intended that sexuality be experienced exclusively in marriage. His Word is full of cautions about lust, sexual fornication, and adultery. Sexual sin is a part of the Ten Commandments: "You shall not commit adultery" (Deut. 5:18).

God sees sex as sacred and holy, having the innate power to bond a husband and wife into a unit to raise godly children. When sexuality is experienced within these proper guidelines, any couple can enjoy great sexual satisfaction.

When I speak at conferences on God's best sex, I am continually floored at how uptight believers are about sex. Just saying the word *sex* from the pulpit can bring all kinds of funny looks. When I share that almost everyone in the Bible had sex, to my amazement I discover that few people have ever even considered such a thing. Many don't think of Moses, Isaiah, and Peter as sexual beings. Even the mother of our

Savior, Mary, had sex with Joseph after Jesus was born and produced other children. Throughout time saints of God have enjoyed sex. Many of them had the same kinds of conversations and experiences with their spouses that you have had. It's liberating to realize that many godly people have enjoyed sexual intimacy!

Where do you believe God is when you are having sex with your partner? When I ask that question at conferences, it surprises people. Does He close His eyes? Does He put black patches over certain areas of your anatomy? No. Of course not! He can see, and He is not ashamed of you or your sexuality. He made it for the both of you to help you to enjoy one another.

God is not hung up about sex. Nothing in the Bible even suggests that God does not want a married couple to have a good time.

God's Best Sex

God's best sex within the marriage relationship is what I call "triune" or "three-dimensional sex." It involves regular physical, spiritual, and emotional intimacy with your spouse. If you do not share spiritual and emotional intimacy yet expect fireworks within your sexual relationship, then you are just kidding yourself. Anything less is simply one-dimensional sex.

One-dimensional, physical sex is what I call "squirt gun" sex. It's simply two bodies having physical sex, but their spirits and souls are not connecting.

Three-dimensional sex is what I call "atomic bomb" sex. The intensity of all three dimensions of your beings touching and experiencing sex is explosive and will make you want to be spiritually and emotionally close regularly. This kind of sex will keep you together for life, and it gets better and better over the years.

If you would like to experience sexual intimacy at a three-dimensional level, follow the three guidelines detailed below (and complete the emotional and spiritual exercises daily).

Principle 1—Eyes open

When you and your spouse are being sexually intimate, keep your eyes open, beholding each other. During sex your brain sends the highest level of endorphins and enkephalins to the excitement center of your brain. It is the highest chemical reward your brain gets for anything. This reward attaches to whatever you are looking at and creates what I call "sex glue." Psychologically you will attach to what you are looking at.

Some couples keep their eyes closed, disconnect, or fantasize about something else during this intimate time of sexual intimacy. This limits their sexual connecting. Sexual connecting is God's will, but your spouse provides what you need to connect. Practice this. It may feel unfamiliar at first, but before long you may begin to experience what some of my clients have called "the best sex of our life!"

Principle 2—Lights on

Keeping some kind of light on during sexual encounters is also important, for it allows you to see each other. If women really understood that whatever a man looks at while having sex is what he bonds to, they would never again feel plagued by concerns over body image. You see, it doesn't matter what imperfections he may see. He will bond to what he looks at. No matter what your body type is, he will like it.

Isn't that great? God knew what He was doing. If you do it right and bond to your wife, thirty years later when she walks into a room with jeans and a T-shirt on, you will say, "Thank You, Jesus!" So I encourage you both to keep some lights on and maintain eye contact.

Principle 3—Nurturing conversation

During sexual intercourse, be as open and vulnerable as you can be spiritually, emotionally, and physically. During this time nurture your spouse with phrases such as, "I love you." "You are special." "You are so handsome." "You are beautiful." "You are a great lover." Such words will go straight into your spouse's very heart of hearts. Sexual intimacy is fertile soil into which to plant the flowers of praise and celebration in your spouse. When you get really good at nurturing each other, the good feelings that flood your spirit and soul will blow you away as your body is being pleasured by your lover and spouse. This is the kind of sexual intimacy God intended.

You won't have to beg your spouse to be sexual if this is the time when you flood him or her with praise. I've never had one client who practiced these three principles during sexual intimacy who ever went back to lights off, eyes closed, and no conversation.

That shut-off type of sexual interaction is "fast-food" sex. It may qualify for sex (food), but it is nothing compared to what you can have. You can enjoy a "five-star meal" with sexual intimacy as you practice these principles during your sexual encounters.

Day 21

THREE DAILY EXERCISES

Pray together? _____ Yes _____ No

What did you pray?

_____

_____

_____

Feelings exercise? _____ Yes _____ No

He shared _____
(feeling #1)

and _____
(feeling #2)

She shared _____
(feeling #1)

and _____
(feeling #2)

165

Praise/nurture together? _____ Yes _____ No

He shared   _____

               (praise #1)

She shared   _____

               (praise #1)

He shared   _____

               (praise #2)

She shared   _____

               (praise #2)

Sexuality: Spouse's turn today is

               husband's _____ wife's _____

Week 3

PROGRESS NOTES

Record your progress for the week on your spiritual exercise of prayer.

Husband:	1	2	3	4	5	6	7
Wife:	1	2	3	4	5	6	7

Record your progress on your feelings exercise.

Husband:	1	2	3	4	5	6	7
Wife:	1	2	3	4	5	6	7

Record your progress on the praise and nurturing exercise.

Husband:	1	2	3	4	5	6	7
Wife:	1	2	3	4	5	6	7

Have you both kept your sexual agreement?

He	Yes	No
She	Yes	No

If no, did that person complete their consequences?

Yes	No

WEEK 4

MAKING THE MARRIAGE
MAKEOVER LAST

Day 22

COMING TO GRIPS WITH FINANCIAL HISTORIES

If any of you lacks wisdom, he should ask God, who gives generously to all without finding fault, and it will be given to him.
—JAMES 1:5

FINANCIAL HISTORIES BEGIN within your family of origin. How your family did or didn't handle money has a major influence on your learning curve about money.

We all bring into our marriages the financial influences from our family of origin. I want to make clear that we cannot blame families for our financial problems. I personally have had to get the information and training to become financially responsible, and anyone else can do the same. There are plenty of Christian books on the subject of finances that you can find in any Christian bookstore.

Your family of origin's influence

Without blaming, you do need to address your family of origin's influence on your financial history.

FAMILY OF ORIGIN FINANCIAL HISTORY

1. How were financial decisions made in your family?

2. Who controlled or managed the money?

3. What were you taught about tithing?

4. What seemed to be the family's attitudes and behaviors about:

   a. Debt?

   b. Large-purchase spending?

   c. Recreational spending?

   d. Saving money?

   e. Investing/retirement?

5. How did your mom and dad communicate about money in general?

6. How did they handle financial crises?

7. What did you learn, both positively and negatively, about money from your parents?

8. In the space below, describe your family's financial influence as best as you can.

   His family's financial influences:

   _____

   _____

   Her family's financial influences:

   _____

   _____

9. You both have financial histories that involve influences from your family of origin. Plan a time with each other to discuss these findings from your family of origin. Our appointment date to discuss this together is:

   _____

You may have a financial history as a single adult prior to marriage. I have prepared some questions for both you and your spouse to help you understand that history. After answering these questions, make a time to discuss these findings.

Financial history of husband prior to marriage

1. As a single person, how did you manage your money?

2. Did you tithe money earned prior to marriage?

3. Did you save money?

4. What was your attitude toward money? Did you consider your money to be your own or God's?

5. How did you pay for your first car?

6. With whom did you discuss money matters, and how did you educate yourself financially prior to marriage?

Financial history of wife prior to marriage

1. How did you as a single person manage your money?

2. Did you tithe money earned prior to marriage?

3. Did you save money?

4. What was your attitude toward money? Did you consider your money to be your own or God's?

5. How did you pay for your first car?

6. With whom did you discuss money matters, and how did you educate yourself financially prior to marriage?

After you are married, you continue to express yourself through your finances, spending, debt, savings, investing, and tithing. Discuss the following questions together as they relate to areas of your past financial history that you would like to change. If money management has been a weak area in your relationship, you may need to ask a pastor or counselor to join you. Some husbands and wives find it helpful to write their answers separately and then to come together in a public place such as a restaurant to discuss them.

Our past financial history

1. As a husband and wife, what have been your beliefs and behaviors regarding tithing?

2. What is your general attitude and behavior toward money? Do you consider it to be God's money or your own?

3. As a couple, what have been your attitudes, behaviors, and agreements about large-purchase spending? Debt? Recreational spending? Savings? Investing? Holiday spending? Budgeting? Retirement?

4. Who primarily manages the money, and why?

5. What have been your financial goals in the past, and have you met these goals?

6. Historically, what emotions arise around the discussion of money? From the husband? From the wife?

After you answer these questions separately, they are to be discussed. See if you can create an accurate account of your financial history together. It is important for you to be aware of how you think about money as a couple. You also need to discern any roadblocks that may be hindering you from experiencing the best intimacy possible.

I realize that some of the issues that you will need to address and not sweep under the rug can be sensitive and challenging. Your journey to intimacy demands self-growth from both you and your spouse in a variety of areas. Be encouraged! Once these major issues are addressed, you will be forever freed from repeating the same past mistakes.

HOW FINANCIALLY GROWN UP ARE YOU?

As individuals, we develop physically, sexually, socially, and financially. How you have grown and developed financially as an individual is vitally important when discussing your financial situation as a couple. You briefly discussed the influence of your family upon your marriage. Now, let's look at how far you have come in your own individual financial development.

Let's outline three stages of development as a financial person.

1. Financial child

A financial child is a husband or wife who absolutely refuses to have anything to do with finances. If you don't say no too often and you give this person his or her candy and toys, he is happy.

An adult who is a financial child feels overwhelmed and confused when money issues are raised. He or she may completely delegate the checkbook to the other spouse and will place the full responsibility of their financial future on the spouse's shoulders. Taxes are too complicated, bank statements don't make sense, and investing is what rich people do, or so the financial child believes.

Financial children live in a magical world where everything seems to work out for their benefit. Christians who are financial children may spiritualize their stunted development by claiming they are "trusting the Lord" to handle the finances. A financial child lives in the here and now only. They do not intelligently address important future financial issues.

This lifestyle can work for the financial child, but eventually the spouse fills with resentment. The burden of shouldering all of the financial concerns, retirement plans, bill payments, and unplanned expenses can be overwhelming. Resentment and disrespect for the financial child

175

can build over the years. Eventually the financial adult's unresolved feelings toward the financial child can erect a roadblock to intimacy.

2. Financial adolescent

A financial adolescent is characterized by an enormous sense of financial entitlement. The money present in the marriage is theirs, regardless of who worked for it. It is not mutual money but "my money." If the financial adolescent wants something, he should have it. Not only should he have it, he should have it "now!"

Financial adolescents never consider the consequences of their purchases. They try to keep up with the Joneses and create a mountain of debt. They want to look good and feel better than everyone around them.

There are dishonest about their spending habits and resent any questions or disapproval of how they manage money. They often punish the more responsible spouse through emotional abuse, withholding sexual intimacy, or becoming even more secretive about their money habits.

The spouse of the male or female adolescent often feels more hopeless than angry. Feelings of aloneness are very real for the man or woman married to a financial adolescent.

3. Financial adult

Few, if any, of us are born as financial adults. Most of us have made our mistakes during our financial adolescence and stumbled into financial adulthood as a result of a tumultuous process. The cost of our financial adulthood education is high, but the results can be tremendous with the time we have left.

Financial adults realize money isn't for them alone. Their money is God's—not only tithes and offerings, but the rest of it as well. They are consciously aware of their stewardship of the money they earn and feel accountable to God for it.

Financial adulthood is distinguished by a genuine effort to be financially responsible. The financial adult is committed to paying bills on time. If that cannot happen, the truth is clearly communicated.

He or she regularly plans for investments, savings, and retirement. Reasonable debt is considered intelligently with pad and paper along with a plan to pay it off. If two financial adults marry each other, they are usually happy and plan together for early retirement and college funds for the children, along with Christmas and recreational spending.

Both husband and wife financial adults share the same values and behaviors. They make informed choices, not based on feelings but on sound financial principles. Secrets are not necessary in a relationship with financial adults. They are able to have firm boundaries financially and accept accountability and seek out wise counsel when needed.

If you are a couple seeking to develop and maintain intimacy on all levels, you must address money issues. This is true whether you are a financial child, adolescent, or adult. Financial agreement must be your next step to intimacy. Only when you aim to live as financial adults can you truly bless each other and your children. God will give you wisdom as you set out on this journey.

Day 22

THREE DAILY EXERCISES

Pray together? _____ Yes _____ No

What did you pray?

_____

_____

_____

Feelings exercise? _____ Yes _____ No

He shared   _____

               (feeling #1)

     and   _____

               (feeling #2)

She shared   _____

               (feeling #1)

     and   _____

               (feeling #2)

Praise/nurture together? _____ Yes _____ No

He shared   _____
                 (praise #1)

She shared   _____
                 (praise #1)

He shared   _____
                 (praise #2)

She shared   _____
                 (praise #2)

Sexuality: Spouse's turn today is

                 husband's _____ wife's _____

Day 23

FINDING FINANCIAL
AGREEMENT

*Suppose one of you wants to build a tower. Will he not first sit down
and estimate the cost to see if he has enough money to complete it?*
—Luke 14:28

W<small>E DISCUSSED ON</small> day 6 the power of the principle of agreement. Well, it is especially powerful when addressing money
matters. Financial disagreement can create much havoc and
pain for a husband and wife. Even if a financial decision wasn't the best,
if a couple agrees together, then they both adjust quite well from an
intimacy perspective.

Money and its issues are part of a learning process, and mistakes will
happen. I don't think I've ever met a couple professionally or personally
who has not made some financial mistakes. If you're expecting not to
make financial mistakes, you may be placing your expectations way too
high.

Can you expect to be informed, wise, and prudent in your money
decisions? Absolutely! Will you be perfect throughout forty or more
years of marriage? Absolutely not! At some point a husband may make
a bad stock decision that causes loss of money. A wife may purchase a
new piece of furniture that costs more than their budget can handle.

So in the process of discussing the principle of agreement, agree that mistakes with money will occur in your lifetime. One partner will forget to deposit a check and the other partner will overdraw the account, or one partner will make a purchase he or she feels is a great deal only to later discover money was lost. Can we agree mistakes will happen?

AGREEING ON FINANCIAL MATTERS

I, _____ , agree with my spouse that financial mistakes will probably happen to us through our lifetime together. (Sign and date)

1. _____ Date _____

2. _____ Date _____

This marks the beginning of your agreement on money matters. I know it may seem like an unusual way to start a discussion on money, but I have encountered too many couples with expectations of financial competency that are too high. Then when the finances are not handled perfectly, scapegoating, blaming, and harmful behaviors can rob the husband and wife of the intimacy God wants them to experience.

I have discovered that God uses finances to teach me faith, to increase my dependence on Him, and to enlarge my relationship with my precious wife, Lisa. We have weathered some interesting storms financially, and some of the storms were not even of our own making. Lisa and I have one steadfast principle that has keep us solid through thick and thin. Lisa and I agree to agree.

We have determined that we will not be in disagreement about any aspect of our financial affairs. We won't spend over a certain amount independently. We won't even increase or decrease our savings or investments or do household improvements without first being in total agreement. If we don't agree, we don't do whatever it is we are thinking about.

I have found that Lisa is God's gift to me in so many areas, and money is one of them. If she is not in 100 percent agreement with a money issue, then we agree that it is not necessary to make that decision yet. If we make a poor decision that we both agreed upon, then we both absorb the consequences without blaming or shaming each other. We both become wiser, and we refine our decision-making process pertaining to money matters.

Let me give you an example about a financial agreement. Every year Lisa and I go out for a New Year's Eve dinner. It is our tradition to set aside that time to review several aspects of our relationship. One of the aspects of our relationship we discuss is our personal financial goals for the new year. We may decide to focus the following year on debt reduction, spending in certain areas, or investments and savings. One year we agreed to pay off all our debts, including our mortgage, which meant that personal spending that year would be kept to a minimum.

Later during that same year I felt a real desire to purchase a new car. My car had been paid off for a few years, and it was about six or seven years old. I started looking at car magazines and would drive by and stop at car dealerships—all the things guys do when they start shopping for a new vehicle. We could definitely afford to buy a car. That was not an issue at that time in our life. But I was forgetting that we had agreed to make no large purchases that year. When my wife reminded me of our agreement, I knew she was right. I didn't like it and may have even argued, but I had given my word and could not break our agreement.

Agreement is primary for navigating through the complexities of money matters. This is why Lisa and I discuss it first, for without agreement, money issues can generate disunity instead of intimacy.

Sign your names below and the date that you agree to agree on your financial journey together for a minimum of one hundred days as you work together toward intimacy.

I agree to agree financially with my spouse.

_____ Date _____

_____ Date _____

ELECTING A MONEY MANAGER

Every husband and wife on the planet has to address the age-old question: Who will manage the money?

Money must be managed through every stage of a couple's marriage. In the early years of marriage, there generally isn't a lot of money to manage. One person might be working and the other attending college. Even if both are working, it doesn't take much to pay the rent for an apartment, perhaps a furniture bill, and a utility or two.

Over time, with increasing mortgages, insurance, and medical expenses for a growing family, the job of managing money can require more time and skill.

Early on couples tend to elect the person who either is naturally better at managing money or the person who puts up less of a fuss about doing it. No election or voting process took place. If you ask most couples when this position was determined, neither will remember the day it began. This entire process of electing a money manager remains a mystery in most marriages.

The person elected into office doesn't realize that this is a lifelong post, and rarely can he or she get a recount of the votes. Everyone just goes along with this pattern for some time. Over time, as this position demands increasing skill in accounting and investing, the money manager can become a lonely position.

The issue of who has authority over the couples' money creeps slowly into the marital dynamic. Surely the person who writes the checks is the authority, right? They miraculously become the financial authority on what can and cannot be purchased and when. True, they have more information, but who voted this person into office anyway?

It's humorous how most couples really don't consider role, authority, and the length of term of the money manager. For some husbands and wives, figuring out who will be the money manager is like a game of hot potatoes. Both partners are anxious to pass it back to the other partner. Neither wants to hold the potato for more than a month or two, or at least until his desired purchase is assured.

You can easily see how manipulation, control, and other issues can naturally arise as a couple determines who will fill the position. Let's briefly look at the money manager's responsibilities, roles, terms, and authority.

Responsibilities of the money manager

- Receives all incoming funds

- Writes checks for all payments due

- Records all transactions

- Reviews monthly bank records to confirm recordkeeping accuracy

- Mails all payments in a timely manner

- Has a reporting system to keep the other spouse informed and updated

- Makes most purchases

- Researches most purchases

- Researches and maintains health, car, house, and life insurance

- Researches and maintains all savings programs for college for the children

- Researches and maintains all investments for the couple

- Plans for Christmas and vacation spending

- Distributes allowances to all family members

- Always is cheerful during financial negotiations

Role of the money manager

- Absorbs all financial stress around debt, spending, and family members' desires

- Does all the job requires without taking away from marital or family time

- Keeps all the details of researching, countless phone hours on hold, and purchase management a secret and puts on a happy face

- Makes sure all family members are content

- Is willing to respectfully and tactfully fight for financial integrity and commonsense spending

Money manager's term of office

- Until death

- Until an accountant, financial advisor, lawyer, or others are hired

- Until other spouse wants a shot at it

- Until the office is shared by both spouses

Authority

- Just under God

- All powerful

- Questionable when the other spouse disagrees

- None whatsoever; the other spouse does whatever he or
  she wants to anyway

We can laugh at ourselves for being willing to take on such a job. Remember, this job is on top of a full-time job and the care of children, and it is a nonpaid position.

OK, I think we have poked enough fun at the position of the money manager. This time you are reviewing the position as a financial adult when you decide who can fill the role of the money manager.

Day 23

THREE DAILY EXERCISES

Pray together? _____ Yes _____ No

What did you pray?

_____

_____

_____

Feelings exercise? _____ Yes _____ No

He shared   _____

        (feeling #1)

   and   _____

        (feeling #2)

She shared _____

        (feeling #1)

   and   _____

        (feeling #2)

Praise/nurture together? _____ Yes _____ No

He shared   _____

          (praise #1)

She shared   _____

          (praise #1)

He shared   _____

          (praise #2)

She shared   _____

          (praise #2)

Sexuality: Spouse's turn today is

           husband's _____ wife's _____

Day 24

RESOLVING KEY MONEY ISSUES

*Then he said to them, "Give to Caesar what is
Caesar's, and to God what is God's."*
—Matthew 22:21

I N THE SPIRIT of the principle of agreement, resolving such issues
as tithing, debt-to-income ratios, preparing for retirement, saving
and investing, and sending kids to college are key to having a relationship with your spouse that is not overstressed by an disorganized
view of finances. Today we are going to flesh out a unified perspective
of money for your marriage so that your intimacy will not be in jeop-
ardy, starting with giving to the things of God.

TITHING

Tithing is an enduring biblical principle in which an individual or
couple gives a tenth of their earnings to the house of God. Theologians
vary in their interpretation of the Scriptures on tithing. However, I will
leave the intellectual issues to others. I am concerned about the heart
of the matter. As we have repeated throughout this guide, agreement
is the core issue. As a first step, get informed by reading Scripture and
books about tithing. Then, more importantly, ask God. Pray and medi-
tate about this matter daily for a week or more, and ask God to give

you a sense of His will for your relationship. As a couple, you can both discern the will of God.

Remember, as Samuel instructed, it is better to obey God than to give sacrifices (1 Sam. 15:22). Your obedience to Christ is the issue. If He has communicated to you as a couple that you should tithe, and you refuse to obey, then you might want to consider James 4:17: "Anyone, then, who knows the good he ought to do and doesn't do it, sins."

This is a major money matter that Christian couples especially must be united in so as not to detract from building intimacy together. Once the issue of tithing is settled by a couple, it will be one less discussion you need to have during the course of your happy marriage.

OUR FINANCIAL COMMITMENT

On this date, _____, Mr. and Mrs. _____
agree to tithe or not to tithe (circle one) _____ percent of their
income to the house of God.

DEBT

Debt is a money matter that every couple needs to address—the sooner the better—so that debt will not become overwhelming.

First, ask yourselves some questions. What are the principles of debt that you both agree upon? God has probably blessed your marriage by giving you both different starting and reference points regarding debt, but where can you find agreement? The following positions (or camps) can help you to clarify what you really believe.

1. Debt is evil. All debt should not happen. If you can't pay for it, you don't need it.

2. Debt is a bad thing but acceptable in the case of a house and/or car purchase.

3. Reasonable debt is acceptable.

4. Debt is a part of life, so do the best you can to stay out of
the bankruptcy court.

5. Purchase as you please. God will clean up any messes that
you make.

How does your camp of agreement line up with your biblical perspective of debt? After prayer, reading, and discussion, agree together on whatever camp you both decide on. Now the question comes to mind, what camp do you actually practice?

As a therapist, I can only believe behaviors. Debt is a behavior that can be traced simply to what you believe about debt. Which camp do you and your spouse operate in? If what you believe and how you behave differ, then you need to develop a plan that is congruent with your convictions. Agreement will be important as you decide on a plan for reducing or incurring future debt.

In the space below, write what you agree upon as far as the principle of debt.

OUR FINANCIAL BELIEF

Our belief about debt as a couple is:

_____

_____

Now that you agree on the principle of debt, let's discuss the percentage of debt you want to have in your relationship.

As a couple, what percentage of your income do you ideally want to have going to pay off debts in your current situation? Look at your debt load right now. How much of your income(s) is going toward debt, mortgage, cars, credit cards, loans, or other large purchase items bought on credit? (circle one)

10 percent   20 percent   30 percent

40 percent   50 percent   Other _____

What is the difference between your ideal percentage of debt and your current percentage of debt? Your answer will give you a place to focus your attention.

Once you have set a goal of what your debt load should be, gather some good reading material on debt reduction and other financial matters, and meet with a financial adviser whom you can trust to help you get your debt-to-income ratio to the percent you have outlined above.

RETIREMENT

All couples will retire eventually unless they go to be with the Lord first. The earlier a couple addresses the issue of retirement, the less stress the marriage will feel. The basics are pretty simple to figure out for a couple: When do you want to retire, and what financial amount do you want to live on?

But in order to effectively and responsibly project into the future what your income needs will be, you will need to enlist the help of a licensed financial advisor. They will be able to help you come up with a strategy that will allow you to meet your goals in timely manner that corresponds to your retirement age and one that is sensitive to the changing market and inflation. Make your commitment below to schedule an appointment with a financial advisor today:

We agree to meet with (name of financial advisor)
_____ from (name of company)
_____ on (date and time of appointment) ___
_____ at (place where you will
meet with him/her) _____.

Like debt, it doesn't matter where you are when you begin. Couples who make a plan about retirement and review this plan at least annually can get in agreement, and it will be one less issue that could potentially block intimacy.

SAVINGS

Keeping an available savings account is a prudent thing to do. Use the principle of agreement to decide how much savings you need as a couple to feel comfortable. This is also something you can bring up when you meet with your financial advisor.

The first savings issue: What percentage of your income do you currently set aside for savings? (circle one)

1 percent   5 percent   10 percent

15 percent   20 percent   Other _____

What percentage of your income do you desire to place in savings? Be sure the amount is reasonable for your current income and lifestyle. Your financial advisor will be able to also give you input as to how much you should put aside in case of job loss, emergency home repairs, replacing furniture, and the like. Once you have come to an agreement, circle one of the percentages below.

1 percent   5 percent   10 percent

15 percent   20 percent   Other _____

The next step is agreeing on when you will begin this savings plan and how it will take place.

The date we are planning to start a savings plan is _____.

The method of savings payments being made is _____.

Now you must agree on the appropriate reasons for making withdrawals from the account. If you are saving for a car and reach the purchase amount, you will experience no discord when you use the funds. On the other hand, if you are saving for a rainy day, and one spouse alone decides to withdraw the money to buy a car or another purchase, disharmony will occur that can disrupt marital intimacy.

As a couple, what is the purpose of your savings? (Remember, this is not a retirement or college fund.)

The purpose of our savings is:

_____

_____

_____

Depending on your governing style, you have determined who has the responsibility or authority to withdraw funds from this account. Do both spouses have access to the records of this account? Do you both have to agree before funds are removed from the account? Do you want to set up an account that requires two signatures to be able to access these funds? These questions must be answered and addressed prior to a "need" that may arise.

COLLEGE

As husband and wife, do you want to fund all, some, or none of your children's or grandchildren's education? Once you agree on whether or not this is a priority, you should create a plan to accomplish this goal financially. Again, talk with a financial advisor about the options available to you and the tax laws surrounding those options. A college education is very expensive, and I don't think we can expect to see the costs go down. The earlier you make the choice the better. As long as you both agree on your position regarding this issue, it should not become a roadblock to intimacy.

BUDGETING

As a couple, given your governing style, have you made a decision in the past to use a budget? Have you stayed within your plans to budget? The decision to design a budget for some couples is very easy. For others it is a real challenge.

PLANNING OUR BUDGET

As a couple, do you agree to formulate a budget in the next few weeks?

❑ Yes   ❑ No

If you do decide to budget, the next issue involves the basics of creating one. Again, I would recommend that you get help from the many good Christian financial books available on the market, a financial advisor, and even taking a budgeting course similar to Dave Ramsey's Financial Peace University or Crown Financial Ministries. This is something you need to act on sooner than later.

Creating a basic budget is a major first step. Write the date below when you compiled your basic budget.

Our basic budget was completed on _____.

A second part of the budgeting process is a regular review. This self-monitoring process is important to regulate charges and have meaningful conversations as you transition through the various money matters that could potentially block future intimacy.

Have at least one monthly business meeting to revise your budget. Schedule this meeting on your calendar. Select a time early in the evening on a weekday. Don't let fatigue become a factor in your discussions. If you agree to this, then place the day and time that best suits your lifestyle and schedule.

> Our regular meeting will take place (circle one) weekly/biweekly/monthly on _____ day of the week at _____ a.m./p.m.

Budgeting is not the most fun thing you can do in a relationship, but it is essential to have open and fact-based financial communication. This type of communication allows for greater intimacy for the couple.

Finances are one of the main areas that can block intimacy. Poor planning, poor communication, and lack of financial agreement can be the archenemy of intimacy. A financial issue can bleed easily over into the emotional and sexual intimacy of a marriage. But don't attempt to try and do all this alone. There are many resources available to help make this process easier. A great and highly recommended start to finding agreement on all the issues mentioned on this day would be to get the input and advice from a licensed financial advisor.

The couple who actively takes on their financial issues is a couple who loves their marriage. Financial maturity, responsibility, and honest communication can protect your great intimate marriage from the needless scarring created by money matters.

Day 24

THREE DAILY EXERCISES

Pray together? _____ Yes _____ No

What did you pray?

_____

_____

_____

Feelings exercise? _____ Yes _____ No

He shared _____

            (feeling #1)

    and _____

            (feeling #2)

She shared _____

            (feeling #1)

    and _____

            (feeling #2)

Praise/nurture together? _____ Yes _____ No

He shared   _____

          (praise #1)

She shared   _____

          (praise #1)

He shared   _____

          (praise #2)

She shared   _____

          (praise #2)

Sexuality: Spouse's turn today is

          husband's _____ wife's _____

Day 25

WINNING THE WAR OF LOVE

*Fight the good fight of the faith....do good... be rich in
good deeds, and... be generous and willing to share.*
—1 TIMOTHY 6:12, 18

G OD KNEW THAT most of us would experience disturbances,
disruptions, or conflict in our relationship with others—and
with our spouses. These are the very elements that allow us
opportunities for growth. These can be opportunities to evaluate your
heart and, hopefully, to mature further into the image of Christ. Unfortunately, some people do not use these challenging opportunities in life
and relationships to mature, but instead they become harder in their
hearts.

Healthy people accept pain as a part of life. They know the question
is not *if* but *when* pain comes into their lives. Now, I don't suggest you
go looking for pain or that you develop a "woe is me" attitude about life.
But it would be wise to acknowledge the presence of pain in your life—
past, present, and future.

Think for a moment about the various relationships you have been
in, including parent/child, husband/wife, teacher/student, peer, family,
or romantic relationships. All relationships that are human have pain.
What makes all the difference in our lives is whether or not we deal

199

with the pain by choosing to work through it to keep the relationship solvent.

Most likely your spouse has disappointed you in the past—and will disappoint you in the future. That's life. You have probably caused some disappointment to your spouse also. Once you accept this, you will no longer respond to pain as a personal affront. This inherent conflict in marriage is part of the process I call *the war of love.*

Being married, you are automatically engaged in this war of love. That doesn't mean that your spouse is the enemy and that you are on the side of justice. No, the war is not about right or wrong—it's about being Christlike and seeking the truth as an opportunity to grow.

You see, you must understand this powerful biblical principle: *if you love, love never fails.* (See 1 Corinthians 13:8.) I like the fact that love never fails, even though I know that I can fail. This knowledge assures me that if I can love, I will learn to fail less and less and will someday win the war of love.

Love is the cornerstone of marriage. The one who loves wins the war. There is no doubt that some days you will find yourself in a battle to love when you feel hurt, misunderstood, tired, or just want to lash out at your spouse. But because of Christ and your love for Him and the love you have for your spouse, you have a much better likelihood of winning than if you ignore the problematic issues in your marriage and attempt to keep love ethereal and intangible. This book has given you tools for wrapping your hands around your marriage and moving it out of the war of love.

PREPARE YOUR BATTLE STRATEGIES

There are some battle strategies that you can use to be successful in your journey through the love agreements.

One battle strategy is called a *blitzkrieg,* which is a simple, powerful, and very effective technique of war. The blitzkrieg technique puts all military forces against one front at a time like a concentrated laser beaming in one direction, moving through the land like an arm sweeping across a table.

What does all this have to do with the marriage makeover you have committed to in this book? *Everything.*

You see, if you generally try to be kinder or to serve your spouse more your way, you may not get long-term results. You will be like a soldier stuck in trenches far from where the battle is taking place. Your ways may be useless for accomplishing the goals you have set for obtaining a truly intimate and fulfilling marriage. A much better plan is to work at ways to be a blessing to your spouse in the blitzkrieg method.

Take all your effort and focus it on one thing. Suppose you are working on being kinder in the way you speak or consider your spouse. Make a plan on how to implement your kindness based on what you've learned about your spouse over the years and during these thirty days. Choose one element of that plan and carry it out, measuring your progress. Stay consistent in that one element of kindness until you think you have achieved your goal. Then take on another goal. Measure that goal, and stay in blitzkrieg mode until you have achieved each goal you set for yourself.

Now you are going to see some real results in your war of love. Keep a log of your progress so that you can see proof that you are actually much kinder today than you were weeks or months ago. Your written notes demonstrate your strategies and the victories you have won.

You are not attacking all fronts at all times but have isolated your efforts to one front at a time. As you secure an area like kindness and hold that ground successfully for a time, then you can move on to the next goal.

In this way you have the practice, discipline, focus, and determination you need to take another part of your territory in the war of love.

Due to changing your behavior from your old *trench tactics*, your spouse is forced to face a growth opportunity. There may be times when he or she faces this new opportunity graciously. But at other times your change may create real conflict.

For example, suppose in your marriage you previously didn't serve your spouse well by doing things around the house. Your lack of service in this area has created a "trench tactic" system, causing your spouse to harbor resentment. You also created an anger-producing situation for your spouse each time the subject of your lack of helpfulness comes up. The shame that would produce in you would distract you from whatever issue you were trying to discuss.

However, with your blitzkrieg maneuver, you have been serving your spouse consistently for several months. Now you are winning the war of love. Your spouse's counterattack of trying to shame and distract you is no longer effective. Obviously it is no longer true that you are not helpful. As a result, your spouse now has an opportunity to grow out of the resentment and anger you formerly caused.

The changes that you make probably will cause some conflict—battle skirmishes. Conflict is inevitable and guaranteed in a marriage relationship if you are actively and intentionally changing from your former "trench tactics" to the more effective "blitzkrieg tactics." When conflict comes, patiently stay consistent. Your consistency is crucial for you to ultimately win the war of love.

Your consistency will bring results. In Galatians 6:9 we read, "Let us not become weary in *doing good*, for at the proper time we will reap a harvest if we do not give up" (emphasis added).

I can't think of anything better than trying to love your spouse more than before. Like a harvest, there is a season of planting and then a season of harvest—and harvest takes time and nurturing.

It will take time for your spouse to trust any new behavior. As time and consistency occur, he or she will begin to trust this new behavior. For some behaviors it may take quite awhile for your spouse to trust that you have actually and sincerely changed. It's at the point of trusting your new behavior that they will decide to change or not. So be patient as you go through the war of love.

KEEP IT REAL

You have embarked upon a pathway for new growth. You will not be perfect on this road of growth. *Stay real, and avoid the "always" and "never" traps.* Neither you nor I are capable of always being loving or perfect and never being imperfect. This is a growth process.

There will be ups and downs in your growth process. Why do I say this? Because you will need to be patient with yourself as you grow. Some days you will be very successful, and you will feel great. Other days in the war of love you might feel like a failure. You may have tried to be patient and kind or to serve, and you just failed. That's life, and it will probably happen again. Don't worry about losing some of the *battles* in the war of love—your goal is to *win the war*! It's important that you maintain your resolve to continue. You'll have the temptation to give up, just as Jesus did.

I'm sure that somewhere along the path of false accusations, beatings, and crucifixion, Jesus might have been tempted to say, "That's enough!" Yet He never lost sight of His long-term goal: "the joy set before him," which was for our salvation. He continued in the battle until He won the war. I want to encourage you to stay in the war of love because it is worth winning.

One area of concern that could cause you to become weary and discouraged is when you start to get frustrated because your spouse is not appreciating "all the changes" you are implementing. After all, you are really working hard, and you start to feel that even if your spouse is not going to change, he or she should at least notice that you are making such a big effort.

This is a tricky trap. As soon as your motivation moves from pleasing Jesus and trying to be more like Him to needing appreciation from your spouse, you can—and probably will—get disappointed, hurt, and discouraged.

When you fall into self-pity or frustration it is usually a sign you want appreciation. Don't look to your spouse to fill your cup; look to Jesus. Hear His voice. He knows how to pour praise into an honest heart that is trying to love His child, your spouse.

Day 25

THREE DAILY EXERCISES

Pray together? _____ Yes _____ No

What did you pray?

_____

_____

_____

Feelings exercise? _____ Yes _____ No

He shared   _____

          (feeling #1)

    and   _____

          (feeling #2)

She shared   _____

          (feeling #1)

    and   _____

          (feeling #2)

Praise/nurture together? _____ Yes _____ No

He shared _____

(praise #1)

She shared _____

(praise #1)

He shared _____

(praise #2)

She shared _____

(praise #2)

Sexuality: Spouse's turn today is

husband's _____ wife's _____

Day 26

DATE YOUR SPOUSE OR GO TO THERAPY!

My beloved spoke, and said to me: "Rise up, my
love, my fair one, and come away."
—SONG OF SOLOMON 2:10, NKJV

FEW THINGS ARE worse than being bored in your marriage. That's why dating your spouse is so powerful, for it can keep your relationship vibrant and freshly energized. Dating is an essential ingredient to a successful and intimate marriage relationship.

Imagine this scene of a wedding. The bride looks beautiful in her white gown and has spent countless hours and thousands of dollars to create a perfect event. She walks down the aisle as the organ plays "Here Comes the Bride." The pastor gives a great sermon about the man and woman becoming one flesh. He asks the groom to say the vows he has written.

The groom says, "I promise to be boring and to bore you all the days of our life. I promise to make you so poor and unimportant that we can never date or get away again."

The bride repeats: "I promise to be boring and to bore you all the days of our life. I promise to make you so poor and unimportant that we can never date or get away again."

Does this sound totally ridiculous? Of course it does. Nevertheless, I have counseled more married couples than I care to remember, and many of them lived lives together that reflected precisely this kind of commitment.

One of my standard questions for a couple is, "How often do you date each other without the children?"

The most common response I receive is, "What do you mean by *date*?" Some want to know if going to the bank, cleaners, and Home Depot counts as a date.

The second most frequent response I am given is, "It's been awhile." When I investigate a little further, I find that it really has been many weeks, months, or sometimes years.

I'll never forget the response of one couple in the early years of my practice. When I asked them when the last time was that they dated, they both looked at each other (which is never a good sign) and agreed it had been at least twenty-two years since they went out together and had fun. I thought they were kidding, but they assured me that it was the honest truth. Of course, being the bright young therapist that I was, I encouraged them to start dating.

Tony and Laura were a smart, young couple in their late twenties. Both were college educated, and both had good careers and bright prospects for their future together. Tony finished law school and was in the beginning of his practice with a law firm. Laura was in the human resources department in a large company downtown. As a young married couple, they went out frequently to dinner, the theater, concerts, and just about anything they could find to do. Time passed, and they had their first child. Laura opted to stay home to be with the baby. Eventually two additional children came along. Needless to say, money was tight as they expanded their family and their expenses. Tony and Laura found themselves in two different worlds.

Tony was busy at work, trying cases and studying to win one lawsuit after another, spending quite a bit of time at the office and bringing paperwork home to do in the evenings. Laura was changing diapers, losing sleep, trying to stay in shape, grocery shopping, going to the cleaners, going to the children's gym classes, taking children to preschool, and active in church functions as well.

They came in for counseling because they were arguing frequently. They honestly didn't feel as if they liked each other very much anymore. He blamed her for being tired and grumpy all the time, and she began attacking him for not being supportive and for being insensitive toward her. As the session went on, I asked about their dating experiences. They both looked at each other and awkwardly laughed. "It's been awhile."

This statement was true. After child number two came along, other than the Christmas party at the office and a few other events, they hadn't dated each other much. I told them that it sounded to me as if they were boring each other to death. Nobody was having fun anymore.

They agreed and started to date every other week while their parents watched the children. This, with a few other adjustments in their marriage, made a huge difference in the quality of their life and intimacy level. They were able to "be" together, not merely function together.

Dating provides an extremely important foundational part of a successfully intimate marriage. I cannot stress the importance enough. You must date if you plan to have a lifelong loving, intimate, and fun relationship.

Friends and acquaintances sometimes ask me, "So how can I improve my marriage and not spend any money to come see you?" It's similar to having a stockbroker or medical doctor as a friend and asking, "Hey, what should I invest in this week?" Or, "Why do I have this pain in this area of my body when I do this, doc?"

I have a simple answer. I simply tell them, "Date your wife."

I am often quoted as saying, "You can either date your wife or go to therapy." Dating is a lot more fun, but if you don't date, you will be speaking to a therapist sooner or later.

Dating is a high priority for Lisa and me. As matter of fact, one of my real motivations for marrying Lisa was to date her permanently and exclusively. She is a fun date, and I love and enjoy the precious time we have together away from the distractions of work and family obligations.

Lisa and I had been married about nine years when our second child,

Jubal, was born. After Jubal was born, Lisa asked if we could stop dating for a while to adapt to being parents to two children. Hadassah, our oldest, was eighteen months, and Jubal was one month old. I agreed, and life went on.

As you may know, having two infants can be stressful. After a few weeks you crave sleep and begin praying to God for just one good night's rest. You're fatigued, but you still have to make it through the day. Week after week went by like this: work, children, sleep, work, children, sleep. You get the picture. Life had no fun in it. Lisa and I were giving of ourselves all our waking hours.

The oil of dating and fun was no longer smoothing out the friction of a busy relationship. The normal stress of work and raising two precious infants was beginning to affect our marriage. I remember driving home one night and realizing that home wasn't fun any more. *What went wrong?* After some thought, I realized we hadn't dated for months.

So, we started dating again, and after two to three weeks our marriage was restored. We were both able to get refreshed, have some fun, and just enjoy each other's company again without the other day-to-day distractions. Since that point we have dated nearly every week.

Let me tell you another story about dating. Many years ago a couple came into my office. Both were in their forties, and they had two teen-aged sons. They came for counseling because they "just weren't getting along." They had been bickering, avoiding each other, and displaying an intolerable level of disrespect for each other. They were considering a separation, but they thought they would try a marriage counselor first.

Typically, each spouse starts out by telling me how bad the other one is during the first few minutes. It's my custom then to ask for a "cease and desist decree" on the blaming. Afterward I take a system check on the marriage.

They both looked disappointed that they couldn't vent all their pent-up emotional poison, but I proceeded in a professional manner.

I asked my first question: "How often do you date each other?"

"Date?" they both asked. "What's that?"

"You know, when you leave the seventeen- and fifteen-year-old at home, and you go have fun together," I explained.

They both glared at me in amazed wonderment and confusion. In Texas they would say, "They looked like a cow staring at a new gate." This couple truly had no reference point for fun or dating in their relationship. They had not gone on a date in nine years.

I explained to them that if you take any two people who love God, love each other, and follow the rules of life in general, but you bore them for nine years and don't let them have a time alone together to rejuvenate, you're going to have two unhappy people. Their first homework assignment was to design two dates, one he would plan and the next one she would plan.

They came back a couple of weeks later. I asked them how it went on their dates. As they told me of the events, I asked them, "So did you have fun?"

They both looked at each other, then at me, and, surprising themselves, said, "Yes, actually we had a lot of fun!" They laughed because earlier they had convinced themselves that they couldn't be together and have fun.

Dating is important, and without it, you will be forfeiting much of the potential that your marriage holds. So let's define what a date is and what it is not.

Dating is simply planning to spend anywhere from three to five hours together—just you and your spouse. Occasionally you may select to do something with another couple, but let that comprise no more than 25 percent of the time. A date is to be a fun time with your spouse, and it is best to have some agreed-upon boundaries for dating.

Day 26

THREE DAILY EXERCISES

Pray together? _____ Yes _____ No

What did you pray?

_____

_____

_____

Feelings exercise? _____ Yes _____ No

He shared _____

(feeling #1)

and _____

(feeling #2)

She shared _____

(feeling #1)

and _____

(feeling #2)

Praise/nurture together? _____ Yes _____ No

He shared _____

(praise #1)

She shared _____

(praise #1)

He shared _____

(praise #2)

She shared _____

(praise #2)

Sexuality: Spouse's turn today is

husband's _____ wife's _____

Day 27

THE RULES

Those who plan what is good find love and faithfulness.
—Proverbs 14:22

THESE BOUNDARIES WILL prove helpful as you develop a dating ritual in your marriage. Use them to protect your dating so that it can last a lifetime for you. Make sure that your dating is safe and fun for both of you so it will have a much greater chance of becoming a fundamental part of your ongoing intimacy together.

1. No problem discussions

Remember, dating is supposed to be fun, and listening to your spouse whine and complain about you is not fun. You can discuss these issues during the other six and a half days of the week. But you must protect your date time from personal problems.

Countless couples tell me that the reason they stopped dating is because it became a gripe session at a restaurant, and they didn't feel like paying a babysitter to be griped at. When you're dating, restrain yourself from sensitive issues. If need be, set a separate night for those conversations, but *not* on the date.

2. No money discussions

Nothing can deflate an evening of fun quicker than saying, "We don't have the money for..." Keep your date evening as free as possible by avoiding any mention of money. You have sixteen hours a day for six days a week to discuss these very important business issues. Don't do it at the time of the week that you get to celebrate your partner.

Some couples may need to schedule a business meeting during the week to discuss all the issues related to finances, children, house, car, future and financial plans, and the business if applicable. This business meeting should be one to two hours long at a separate time from dating so that the issues don't bleed into your dating time.

3. No errands

Dating is not a time to trap your spouse in a car and go to Target, Home Depot, the cleaners, or the bank. Running errands is not dating.

Errands are an essential part of every busy family. If you need to divide and conquer during the week or on the weekends, ordain an errand evening in which the family does them together. But whatever you do, guard your valuable dating time from errands. It will pay off in the long run.

4. Limit shopping

Ladies, most men don't like shopping, and not too many women want to spend a romantic evening in the power tool aisle at Home Depot. Shopping falls under the category of errands. Now, some couples may decide to use a date night to do some Christmas shopping, but I really caution couples against shopping dates in general.

Shopping dates can also trigger one of those "if we only had the money" conversations. If you do agree to shop, really make sure that both of you are in 100 percent agreement that this is the way you want to spend your special night.

Maintaining these basic boundaries will insure positive dating experiences. Not every date will be perfect, but keeping these boundaries in place will help. You will not only be paying for a movie or dinner, but you will also be paying a babysitter. With so much money invested, make sure it will be as positive an experience as possible.

How Often?

In keeping with the principle of agreement, you both will need to agree about the details of dating. Honoring your governing style, circle your agreed-upon frequency in the space below.

Weekly   Two times a month   Once a month

Many couples agree to date but neglect to nail down their commitment to the details, and therefore they don't follow through. Together as a couple, determine the best day for you to date, considering both of your schedules. Please circle the day that works best for both of you.

Mon.   Tues.   Wed.   Thurs.   Fri.   Sat.   Sun.

The next issue to agree upon is the time. You can date in the morning, noon, or night. It's totally up to both of you. The time isn't important, but the commitment to make it a consistent time is very important. As a couple, fill in the below space with the best time for you to date.

_____ a.m./p.m.

The last decision to make is agreeing to a start date. So in the space below write the date you would like to implement your dating ritual.

Our dating shall commence on _____.

Great! You have made real progress on this very important ritual. In the space below, write out your dating agreement for future reference.

OUR DATING AGREEMENT

Mr. and Mrs. _____ have agreed to date on a
_____ basis, commencing on the day of our Lord Jesus
Christ _____ in the year _____. As often as
humanly possible, this date shall begin at _____ a.m./p.m.

Agreeing to date will breathe a breath of fresh air into your marriage. Many of my most precious memories of my marriage are from our date nights. I really pray the Lord's richest blessings on this time of dating for you both, and may He confirm to you the blessedness of this tradition in your marriage.

WHO IS RESPONSIBLE?

Who will be responsible to decide what we do during our date?

Let me offer the single best solution that I have found from working with couples for applying dating responsibility: each spouse must be 100 percent responsible 50 percent of the time.

Let me clarify what I mean by 100 percent responsible. On the night of the date, one person decides, without being influenced by the other partner, where they are going and what they will do. Now, the next time they date, the other spouse will be 100 percent responsible to choose where they go and what they do.

The expectations and benefits are clear in this system. You always know who is responsible, and you never have to play table tennis with the question, "What do you want to do?"

The responsibility of the person who chooses the date is to decide upon an outing that is fun for *himself* or *herself*. The objective is for the responsible person to have a really good time. In this arrangement, you are *not* trying to make the *other person* happy.

You can never make someone else happy. It is totally your spouse's responsibility to make himself or herself happy. Besides, your partner will get a chance to make himself or herself happy next week.

This is the fairest system of them all. You both get to choose your date. You have plenty of time to come up with something creative for yourself, and you need not feel any false guilt, because your spouse gets a fair shot at it the following date.

Date designers, your only responsibility is to be sure that your spouse knows what to wear. You don't want your partner showing up at a ballet in shorts or wearing good slacks to go skating. You do not have to tell your spouse where you're going or what you're doing until you get there. Life is an adventure!

Before we go any further, let's discuss the role of the spouse who is *not* designing the date. You are the guest, and you simply are going along for the ride. You may or may not even know where you are going. The guest's role is to be *a happy camper* and to go through the date with grace. You are to love and celebrate your spouse during this event and to make it as positive as possible.

I encourage you to create your own rotation dating system so that you can increase and maintain your intimacy for a lifetime.

Day 27

THREE DAILY EXERCISES

Pray together? _____ Yes _____ No

What did you pray?

_____

_____

_____

Feelings exercise? _____ Yes _____ No

He shared   _____

               (feeling #1)

    and   _____

               (feeling #2)

She shared   _____

               (feeling #1)

    and   _____

               (feeling #2)

Praise/nurture together? _____ Yes _____ No

He shared _____

(praise #1)

She shared _____

(praise #1)

He shared _____

(praise #2)

She shared _____

(praise #2)

Sexuality: Spouse's turn today is

husband's _____ wife's _____

Day 28

MAKING IT HAPPEN

The plans of the diligent lead to profit as surely as haste leads to poverty.
—PROVERBS 21:5

I HAVE USED THE term *babysitters*. But it really does not adequately reflect the value of a good sitter to a married couple. Lisa and I have no family living nearby, so we've been forced to search diligently for just the right person, a conscientious individual who would make our children feel comfortable. The young people who have come alongside of us have been nothing less than a ministry to us.

Angels are seen ministering to Jesus after His forty-day fast. The Bible says that angels minister to the heirs of salvation: "Are not all angels ministering spirits sent to serve those who will inherit salvation?" (Heb. 1:14). The young ladies who have ministered to our children on a weekly basis have been angels to us. Our blessing of intimacy is a by-product of their service to our marriage and our children. Years later our children still talk about Britney, Erica, Liz, and Corrie.

Angel-sitting is a ministry, which is why I use this term, not because my children were angels. I use the term because it elevates the service of these young people to the place of honor it should have.

Of course, the person you choose to watch your most precious gifts, your children, should be mature and responsible. Here is some practical advice:

1. Always pay your angel-sitters well. A minister is worth his or her wages according to 1 Timothy 5:18, which states, "The worker deserves his wages." These young ladies serve you, and the good ones are in high demand in every church and neighborhood.

2. Always go the extra mile to communicate your expectations. Be sure you have clearly instructed your sitters about such things as feeding times, playing crafts or games with your children, boundaries around answering the door, having friends stop by, and what types of entertainment are acceptable. Clearly communicate these boundaries in writing. The clearer the communication, the more relaxed your date will be.

3. Respect your angel-sitter's schedule. If your sitter has to switch a day, be gracious to oblige when you can.

4. Be overly responsible. If your sitter is walking home or driving home, communicate with your sitter's parents and be sure she returns home safely after watching your children.

5. If you are planning Christmas and New Year's Eve events, plan at least a month or two ahead and get a firm commitment. Remember to pay more on holidays, because all other jobs get paid more on the holidays.

6. Always verbally affirm to your sitters how important they are. Personally, I go out of my way every single time to say how much I appreciate them. Their being able to sense that they mean a lot to you goes a long way in building loyalty.

Remembering that these young people, friends, or family members are angels ministering to you and your children can help you to esteem them as highly as they deserve. Without angel-sitters, dating is impossible, so they are valuable people colaboring with you to have the utmost of intimacy in your marriage.

PLAN FINANCIALLY

Paying your angel-sitter as well as paying for your dating activities and meals can add up quickly. To make dating more relaxed, sit down with your spouse and briefly go over what you can currently afford to spend for a date. If you have a household budget already in place, include dating. In addition, discuss who will make the trip to the bank to prepare for the date. An easy method is having the person who is in charge of the date make sure the funds are available prior to the date.

Money spent on dating is money well invested, but it is still money spent. Using the principle of agreement within your governing style, discuss your financial boundaries for dating. In this way, both of you will be aware of the maximum amount you will spend on a date. Money talk will have less opportunity to place a damper on your date.

Dating isn't about how much money you spend. Some of my dates with Lisa cost absolutely nothing. Others have cost less than ten dollars. It is important, however, that you agree on what can be spent, excluding the angel-sitter.

The amount that you both believe you can agree on is:

$ _____ amount

minus $ _____ for angel-sitter

equals $ _____ total to be spent on a date

ARE YOU COMMITTED?

Although dating is fun, it is also a real commitment. I want to encourage you both to keep your commitment to dating, for it is a very holy commitment. Our friends know that Lisa and I are not available on our date night. We are committed not to schedule anything on our date night. To reschedule, we both must fully agree to sacrifice a date for whatever reason. Neither husband nor wife solely has the authority to decide to disrupt a date night.

I want to illustrate my personal commitment to dating. There was a time when our only sitter lived thirty minutes away from our house. It took us a total of two hours in the car to pick her up and drop her off because she did not have a car. But I made this two-hour drive for more than a year so that we could date. That's a commitment!

I realized that if my wife and I didn't feel the children were safe, then dating would not be fun. But having Britney as our angel-sitter gave us a sense of assurance and peace so that we were free to enjoy our date.

Dating isn't only great for you, but it is also great for your children.

WHAT ABOUT THE CHILDREN?

Consistent dating sends a strong message to your children about the value of marriage. Our children will learn from what we do, not merely what we say. I want my son, Jubal, to celebrate and date his wife throughout his life. I also want my daughter to marry a man who will not bore her to death but will celebrate her through dating.

If I don't want my children to end up in marriage counseling, I must consistently demonstrate the importance of dating.

I remember once when Hadassah was three years old and Lisa and I were leaving for a date. She said, "Daddy, I want to go with you." With that she gave one of these desperate little faces only a daughter can give.

I bent down, looked into her eyes, and said, "Daddy loves Mommy with his whole heart, and I want to take her out tonight." Hadassah's big brown eyes lit up, and she smiled a big and happy grin as she walked up the stairs to be with our angel-sitter.

I don't know exactly what Hadassah was thinking, but she never asked again to go out on our date night. If you're just starting to date and your children are a little older, you may face some resistance because it is unfamiliar to them. Weather the storm, and they will soon accept your evenings out.

My daughter and son understand dating as a regular, normal part of marriage. Some day I hope to teach our grandchildren to maintain the tradition on a weekly basis. It's not what you believe about marriage that your children will repeat; it's what you *do* in your marriage.

Personally, I believe that our children desperately need a break from us just as much as we need a break from them. They need to experience different personalities. They need that time of eating pizza and popcorn and doing what they want without Mom and Dad hovering over them.

Our children love their angel-sitters. When we tell them Corrie is coming, they get so excited. All day long they will question us about her arrival. It has become a special time for them too.

We have covered dating very thoroughly so that you can effectively implement this very important tradition into your relationship. Briefly, I would like to explore one more aspect of dating: discovering what you like to do on your date.

Day 28

THREE DAILY EXERCISES

Pray together? _____ Yes _____ No

What did you pray?

_____

_____

_____

Feelings exercise? _____ Yes _____ No

He shared   _____

               (feeling #1)

    and   _____

               (feeling #2)

She shared   _____

               (feeling #1)

    and   _____

               (feeling #2)

Praise/nurture together? _____ Yes _____ No

He shared   _____

            (praise #1)

She shared   _____

            (praise #1)

He shared   _____

            (praise #2)

She shared   _____

            (praise #2)

Sexuality: Spouse's turn today is

            husband's _____ wife's _____

Day 29

IDEAS FOR DATING AND OTHER FUN GETAWAYS

Come away, my lover, and be like a gazelle or like a
young stag on the spice–laden mountains.
—SONG OF SOLOMON 8:14

ALTHOUGH IT IS tempting to give you an exhaustive list of ideas for dating, I will resist. If you need some ideas, browse through your local bookstore. I am more interested in discovering what dates you as individuals would like to experience. Remember, dating is for you to have fun. It's not to try to guess what would make your spouse happy. So on a separate piece of paper, I want both of you to record date ideas that you think would be fun.

Now that you have created a list on dating, two questions remain. Whose dating idea will be first, and when will you start? In my office, we simply flip a coin. The winner of the first toss starts the dating process. Record your winner by circling *husband* or *wife* on the following chart.

DATING BEGINS

Husband   Wife

Together, quickly decide when dating should start. Record that date: _____.

You are well on your way. I pray God's richest blessings upon you both as you invest in each other's hearts and interests. As you celebrate the spouse God has given to you, I pray that you experience a deeper sense of intimacy during these thirty days.

Every couple needs to have fun to create a depth to intimacy throughout marriage. Before children arrive, having fun gives you something to do with all the extra energy you have, and it helps you to create new avenues of interest. As you move into the active child-raising years, the need for fun increases, because now you need to recharge yourself and escape the daily stress. As you mature, you need fun to maintain interest in the activities that will be essential for a stable retirement.

What I'm talking about is the one-, two- or three-day getaways that are not for the entire family, but only for you and your spouse. Where you go is not nearly as important as the fact that the two of you are together. Some couples choose a weekend at a hotel in the next city, a cabin in the woods, or a cottage on the beach. This is unscheduled time together where the greatest decision is, "What's for lunch?" You can shop, eat, sleep, or just relax together.

Soaking in fun, fellowship, and refreshment can be one of the richest investments you can make in your marriage. Fun can revitalize a marriage like nothing else. Occasionally Lisa and I visit a very large hotel in Dallas. This hotel has three pools, a large gym, and five restaurants. We park our car on Friday and don't drive anywhere the entire time. Such long weekends can feel like a two-week vacation together. We come back replenished with more to give to our children and our work.

Fun must be scheduled. Some couples have a knack for regular fun, spontaneity, and creativity. Most of us, however, really need to plan for it. Hopefully, your marriage will outlast your career and the days in which your children are at home. Therefore, have fun with your spouse. The returns on this investment are worth the money you spend, even if you have to save to do so.

PLANNING A GOOD TIME

What issues do you need to walk through to make fun a part of your marriage? How often do you want to plan for fun?

What is reasonable for you to do for fun in a year? You might choose to schedule a getaway annually, biannually, or quarterly if you can afford it.

As a therapist, I encourage you to try to get away at least annually. It could keep you looking forward to something for a long time. Personally, I was able to get through some very tough work schedules because I knew our weekend together was coming up.

Using the principle of agreement within your governing style as a couple, discuss what you think your frequency of fun getaways could possibly be this year. After you have agreed upon the frequency for fun, please circle your decision for this below:

    Annually   Biannually   Quarterly

As a couple, discuss your financial ability to plan for this expenditure. Saving twenty dollars a month over a year can pay for a weekend stay at a hotel in most cities. It's important that you both agree on this. It will be a lot less fun if you spend your entire time worrying how much all of it is costing. Together, discuss the cost of what you circled above. Below, please fill out your agreed-upon spending per occurrence:

$ _____ per fun getaway

times the number of fun getaways _____

equals $ _____ total annual spending for fun getaways

229

If you have a budget, fun getaways together with dating could become line items. Having a strong, intimate marriage costs money, just as having a healthy body or increasing wealth takes money. So long as you remain in agreement, then fun can remain fun.

What would you like to do for fun? Each person in a relationship may consider different kinds of getaways to be fun. One person may want to go skiing, and the other desires a weekend in a cabin somewhere. Here again, be sure to honor both of you. If you only have fun in one manner, then only one person is being fulfilled.

Some couples have used the same system for fun that they use for dating. They create a rotating system. Each person takes a turn being responsible for planning the fun that they want to have. The other spouse's role is to be a happy camper. In this way, both of you get a fair shake at having fun. As you discuss this, if you would like to rotate fun times between the both of you, indicate it below:

Agree to rotate   Only one person decides

After deciding how often, how much, and who will be responsible for the fun, there is only one thing left to decide. You must individually decide what you would like to do for fun.

Decide beforehand what you would like to do so you will be motivated to follow through.

PLACES TO GO

Decide who should take the first turn. Flipping a coin works well for this too. The winner is the first spouse to start the fun assignment. Record your decision.

Husband   Wife

The last phase of planning fun requires a calendar. Together I would like you to look at it and see what days are feasible for this fun event(s). Below record your agreed-upon date(s) for fun this coming year.

Mr. and Mrs. _____ commit to _____ days
in the month(s) of _____ and _____, including the
dates of _____, _____, _____.

Now, go have a great time! Discover that the spouse God gave to
you is a blessing from Him. During your planned fun, I pray that you
remember the reasons you first married. I pray that God refreshes your
intimacy—spiritually, emotionally, and physically. So enjoy yourselves
and make your friends jealous over the great relationship you have redis-
covered with your spouse.

Day 29

THREE DAILY EXERCISES

Pray together? _____ Yes _____ No

What did you pray?

_____

_____

_____

Feelings exercise? _____ Yes _____ No

He shared   _____

            (feeling #1)

    and   _____

            (feeling #2)

She shared   _____

            (feeling #1)

    and   _____

            (feeling #2)

Praise/nurture together? _____ Yes _____ No

He shared   _____

         (praise #1)

She shared   _____

         (praise #1)

He shared   _____

         (praise #2)

She shared   _____

         (praise #2)

Sexuality: Spouse's turn today is

            husband's _____ wife's _____

Day 30

CELEBRATE EACH OTHER
FOR A LIFETIME

The LORD your God is with you, he is mighty to save.
He will take great delight in you, he will quiet you with
his love, he will rejoice over you with singing.

—ZEPHANIAH 3:17

W HEN YOU CELEBRATE your spouse, you are in agreement
with God. You are exhibiting your Christlikeness when you
are singing the same song of celebration over your spouse
that God sings.

Pause for just a moment; does your spouse feel celebrated? Would he
or she be able to say, "My spouse celebrates me so much"?

Don't be tempted to slide into a little, "What about me? My spouse
doesn't celebrate me." Instead, you lead in the party to celebrate your
spouse. Choose to plant celebration in your spouse's life. Everyone loves
a party! Once you start celebrating, the atmosphere of your relationship has some change—and that's the change in you. You will change
and begin to pick up, maintain, or make louder the celebration of your
spouse.

It may be that some of those great characteristics in your spouse about
which you bragged before marriage may have begun to appear as weak-

nesses. Before marriage you may have thought your spouse was *thrifty*, but now you would call it *cheap*. Once you thought your spouse to be so *smart*, but now he or she comes off as a *know-it-all*. By now I'm sure the list could go on and on about the weaknesses you see in your spouse.

Think honestly about this: *Has your spouse changed so much, or has the way you think about your spouse changed?* With many couples, it is how we think about our spouse that has changed more than the changes in our spouse. We go from a spirit of celebration to a spirit of criticism toward our spouses.

Remember that criticism of another believer in Christ will probably place you on the wrong side of God. He is not a criticizer of your spouse but a celebrator. I like to always be on the same team as God. If I continue to celebrate Lisa, regardless of her disposition or actions, I am in agreement with God.

HOW DO I CELEBRATE MY SPOUSE?

Let's consider some of the different ways you can celebrate your spouse.

To the Father

One of the greatest ways to celebrate your spouse is in the presence of his or her Creator. Spend time on a regular basis just praising God for your spouse.

Celebrate the fact that God gave your spouse to you. You can praise Him for how blessed and different you are because your spouse is in your life. Praise God for his or her attractiveness, sexuality, personality, humor, friendship, and any other attributes you want to highlight to the Father.

Remember that not only is God your Father—He is also your Father-in-law. Now I don't know about for you, but if I start bragging about my wife in front of her earthly father, he smiles. If a human father-in-law likes to hear good things about his child, so does your heavenly Father-in-Law. He loves to hear you praise Him for your spouse. Try it sometime.

As a matter of fact, you can try it right now. Put down this book, and, for the next two or three minutes, get alone with God and thank Him for your spouse. Celebrate your spouse before the living God. See what happens.

If you stopped and praised God, I'll bet you can feel His smile. I always feel His smile when I praise Him for Lisa.

To the enemy

I know I have your attention now. What could I possibly mean when I say to celebrate your spouse in front of the enemy? When I say the enemy, I mean the devil and any of his demons that might want to highlight your spouse's weaknesses.

They start by suggesting negative thinking about your spouse. You know the mantra, "Your spouse is selfish, insensitive to your needs, lazy, arrogant, willful, and rebellious." The list never seems to stop. The enemy's objective is to utilize your relationship with your spouse to cause you to hurt, criticize, or emotionally abandon him or her. The enemy knows that your spouse is the closest person to your heart. If he can get you to buy into his lies and criticisms, *whammo*, his work is done. Your creativity and resources take over, and you begin to belittle and demean your spouse yourself.

According to the Bible, the devil is the accuser or criticizer of those who are saved (Rev. 12:10–11). Never forget that the enemy hates your godly spouse and the other parent of your children because together you are raising godly seed for the future battles of the kingdom.

I have learned that the best way to deal with the enemy's lies to me about my spouse is to celebrate her continually. There is great power in celebrating your spouse. You can utilize this power to fight *for* your spouse instead of *against* him or her, and you will truly be a winner at marriage.

To others

Celebration in the presence of others is powerful. Celebrate your spouse in front of everyone. Your spouse is wonderful; that's why someone as smart as you married him or her. Tell your children privately and publicly in front of your spouse what you like, love, admire, appreciate, and depend upon in your spouse. Let your spouse and your children know that you benefit greatly because your spouse is alive and married to you.

Tell your parents, their parents, your neighbors, and friends about the goodness and value of your spouse. Do this when you are alone with these people. Make others believe that you are blessed because you are married to your spouse. You are the president of your spouse's fan club, so let others know about the ongoing celebration of your spouse.

To your spouse

Celebrating your spouse directly is a very important aspect of celebration. You can celebrate your spouse with consistent, little gifts to demonstrate your love and appreciation. At times a handwritten card is the best way to celebrate your spouse. Surprise him or her with a favorite coffee, tea, juice, or soft drink. Take your spouse to a favorite restaurant for a long lunch, buy them a gift certificate to a spa for a massage, or get them tickets to their favorite sporting event.

Another way to send a clear message of celebration is spending *quality time together* doing something your spouse really likes to do. This sends a clear message that you really celebrate this aspect about him or her. If your spouse loves to ski, even if you are not a great skier, you can go, drink hot chocolate, and listen to the ski stories as a way of celebrating how God made your spouse.

Another very important way to celebrate your spouse is through your spoken words. It would be hard to overestimate the power of your words. To prepare to celebrate your spouse with your words, list several things you like about your spouse.

Find a way to articulate each thing on the list to your spouse. For example, if you listed that you like your spouse's work ethic, you could say, "You know, I was thinking about you today, and I realized again how industrious you are. You really like to accomplish things, and I really like that about you."

WHAT I LIKE ABOUT MY SPOUSE

1. _____
2. _____
3. _____
4. _____
5. _____
6. _____
7. _____
8. _____
9. _____
10. _____

Now for each of the things you listed, write a corresponding sentence of celebration that you can express to your spouse.

1. _____
2. _____
3. _____
4. _____
5. _____
6. _____
7. _____
8. _____
9. _____
10. _____

To yourself

This is where celebration can become really important. This is a really good way to keep your celebration of your spouse going. Stop for a moment and evaluate some ways that God has made your spouse *better* than you. Just as there are some strengths that you have that your spouse does not have, so too he or she will have strengths that you do not have.

Think about some ways in which God made your spouse better than you. List some of these strengths on the lines below.

WAYS MY SPOUSE IS BETTER THAN ME

1. _____
2. _____
3. _____
4. _____
5. _____
6. _____
7. _____
8. _____
9. _____
10. _____

If you cannot think of strengths to list, you may need to make celebration of your spouse a priority in your life. So try hard, dig deep, and fill out ten ways that your spouse is better than you.

The fact that he or she is better than you in specific areas doesn't take away from the wonderful strengths that you possess. It just helps you to focus on your spouse and his or her own wonderful qualities.

I find that keeping this list around until it gets into the heart is helpful. When you can see your spouse's strengths, it is much easier to celebrate your spouse both to yourself, God, others, and the enemy.

Now that you are armed with the power of celebration, you can make celebrating your spouse a naturally occurring part of your relationship so that the atmosphere and the dynamics in your marriage begin to transform into a harmonious, intimacy-filled union.

Day 30

THREE DAILY EXERCISES

Pray together? _____ Yes _____ No

What did you pray?

_____

_____

_____

Feelings exercise? _____ Yes _____ No

He shared _____

        (feeling #1)

  and _____

        (feeling #2)

She shared _____

        (feeling #1)

  and _____

        (feeling #2)

Praise/nurture together? _____ Yes _____ No

He shared _____
(praise #1)

She shared _____
(praise #1)

He shared _____
(praise #2)

She shared _____
(praise #2)

Sexuality: Spouse's turn today is

husband's _____ wife's _____

Week 4

PROGRESS NOTES

Whose responsibility was it to plan a date this week?

    His   Hers

Rate your date (the spouse who planned it).

    1   2   3   4   5   6   7   8   9   10

Did you stick to the rules on dating?

He	Yes	No
She	Yes	No

Record your progress for the week on your spiritual exercise of prayer.

Husband:	1	2	3	4	5	6	7
Wife:	1	2	3	4	5	6	7

Record your progress on your feelings exercise.

Husband:	1	2	3	4	5	6	7
Wife:	1	2	3	4	5	6	7

Record your progress on the praise and nurturing exercise.

Husband:	1	2	3	4	5	6	7
Wife:	1	2	3	4	5	6	7

Have you both kept your sexual agreement?

He   Yes   No

She   Yes   No

If no, did that person complete their consequences?

Yes   No

This week did you work on your financial goals? Record your individual progress.

Husband: 1   2   3   4   5   6   7

Wife: 1   2   3   4   5   6   7

Conclusion

GO FORWARD

YOU ARE ABOUT to take a fantastic journey of change. You are on a journey to be more Christlike than ever before. This journey will require radical shifts in your thinking and behavior.

You are now more informed than many on how to honestly change the dynamics in your marriage. You are the power of one who decides if change should occur. Throughout these thirty days, you have been asked to accept any flaws your spouse might have. You learned to concentrate your attention on yourself in order to become a great influencer in your marriage.

You have been taught the important principle of the power of the seed. You know that the Spirit of God in you is already faithful, patient, forgiving, serving, respectful, kind, and celebrating. This seed is in you.

You just have to let this seed out of you and grow all the fruit that you want your spouse to taste. As he or she tastes over and over the godly fruit hanging on your tree, your spouse will begin to trust that a continual harvest of fruit will be available to him or her.

The love agreements will teach you this critical principle: believe your behavior. As you look at your behavior, you are much more likely to be intentional and successful.

You also learned the importance of having specific goals that you measure consistently. This is a powerful principle in your growth process. As you learn to add accountability to each love agreement, you are almost assured of victory.

Ecclesiastes 4:9–10 reveals the principle that "two are better than one, because they have a good return for their work: If one falls down, his friend can help him up. But pity the man who falls and has no one to help him up!"

As you go into battle, you are not going alone. No army sends a soldier out to battle alone. One of the first things that happen to a recruit in boot camp is for him to be assigned a buddy. His buddy is there to pick him up if he gets wounded, and he is there for his buddy as well.

Be encouraged that this is a great journey. It is a journey you don't have to wait for your spouse to take with you. You take the journey, and maybe your spouse will come along later.

Don't be discouraged; your spouse may not change immediately. If your spouse is not intentionally trying to become more Christlike, it may be awhile. He or she may see no need to change and may be content at the level of Christlikeness he or she has reached with little effort. Leave that to Jesus. You just push forward practically and intentionally.

Like a mother eagle, I am at the point of pushing you out of the nest to fly. As you jump and go, you will experience your spiritual wings in a grand new way.

You will soar in Christ like no other time in your life. I live in Colorado, and we go to a place in the mountains where bald eagles live. To watch a bald eagle fly is absolutely amazing. You literally stop what you're doing to watch. You pull your car over and just watch in amazement at the flight of the eagle.

That is what you want your spouse to see in you—the flight of an eagle. Give him or her a chance to see faithfulness, patience, forgiveness, service, respect, kindness, and celebration soaring every day in his or her life.

Your spouse needs to have the time to stop and drink in these experiences of your love agreements. Soar, and let him or her watch. If your spouse chooses to join you in flight, that's great. If not, you are the power of one enticing others to the great flight of becoming more like Jesus.

May God bless your flight.

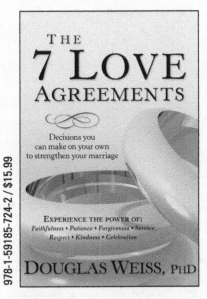